STORIES from Raven Rock NEW JERSEY

STORIES *from* Raven Rock NEW JERSEY

EDITED *by* R. CURT CHINNICI

THE History PRESS

Published by The History Press
Charleston, SC 29403
www.historypress.net

Cover images: Front courtesy of Gratz Gallery, Doylestown, Pennsylvania. Rear drawing by author. Rear painting courtesy of Betty Schuck Davis.

First published 2012

Manufactured in the United States

ISBN 978.1.60949.835.1

Library of Congress CIP data applied for.

Contents

Preface

The story of Raven Rock is typical of many small villages in New Jersey: natural resources were plenty and were then exploited by early Americans; fast growth took place due to improved means of transportation; land speculation occurred; natural disasters were present; and finally, the eventual decline into a sleepy hamlet took place. Raven Rock's story is unique in that it maintained its small size even though its various enterprises caused periods of economic growth. Raven Rock's geographic location on the Delaware River connected it with its sister community, Lumberville, Pennsylvania, on the other side of the river. The bridge or ferry crossings allowed community members to conduct social and business activities on both sides of the Delaware. The railroad connected it to points north and south. What kept it isolated and "protected" was the poor condition of the roads leading to it until just 60 years ago. This isolation made it an ideal spot for artists to work undisturbed. A new road made it accessible for recreational activities, and soon thereafter, a state park was developed here. Of course, the people who lived here added drama and humor to the events that occurred during the first 250 years of the history of Raven Rock.

—R. Curt Chinnici

Acknowledgements

The authors and editor would like to thank the following people and institutions: Dennis Bertland; Troy Bianchi; Suellen Bock; Birgita Bond of the Michener Museum; Mick Byers; Don Cornelius at the Hunterdon County Historical Society (HCHS); Luverne Updegrove Caulton for pictures and hours of sharing her memories of the people and events of Raven Rock; Betty Schuck Davis for preserving and sharing information and pictures of historic significance to Raven Rock; Tim Davis for making introductions and preservation of local artifacts; Ethel Emmons; Robert Goodwin; the Hunterdon County Historical Society; the Hunterdon County Cultural & Heritage Commission; Sue (Thelma) Kintzel; Doug McMichael; the Michener Museum of Art; Paul W. Schopp; the Tinsman family of Lumberville; Floyd Updegrove; and Sam Waugh.

We wish to thank the owners of the dwellings described in this book for their kindness in allowing us to document their historic structures. These families include: Foley, Zdepski, Antonelli, Ripley, Ciarrocca, Saja, Strober, Chinnici, Adams, Oliveras, Nicklen, Fisher, Reynolds, Kellogg, Wright, Karsan and Dorko, as well as caretakers Eva, Sheri, Rose and Sandy.

And we also wish to thank those who have recorded and promoted Raven Rock during their lives: B.A. Sorby, historian and preservationist; Egbert T. Bush (1848–1937), historian and contributor to the *Hunterdon County Democrat*; and Edna Mason Laszlo.

Introduction to Raven Rock, New Jersey

Geoffrey A. Nicklen

Today, Raven Rock, New Jersey, can be easily reached using Route 29, a broad and fast highway, by heading north out of Stockton or south from Frenchtown. One may not even notice a handful of old houses just outside the Bull's Island State Park. Raven Rock is hardly a village, as it has no store or any kind of business: just a dot on a busy highway in Delaware Township, Hunterdon County, New Jersey.

It wasn't always this way. Going back in time, Bull's Island was an isolated place. Early on, this remote one-mile-long island was reachable only by a Native American path. Later, early colonists improved the dirt lane, and now it is called Quarry Road. Afterward, access was by a canal, then a railroad and finally by State Route 29.

Long forgotten are the Native Americans who fished and hunted deer on the banks of the Delaware River and Bull's Island. They came and camped using trails that descended from higher land above the river valley. Life remained this way until the white man came. The sharp-eyed, land-hungry agents of the Crown soon rid the area of the Leni-Lenape Indians. They had one hundred years of experience in taking Indian lands using parchment documents and the persuasion of strong drink.

New Jersey and Pennsylvania were well settled by this time. Bull's Island and Raven Rock were developed later due to their remoteness. The first white owners of the island, Richard Bull and John Ladd, men of privilege and connections, gained deed to 625 acres that included the

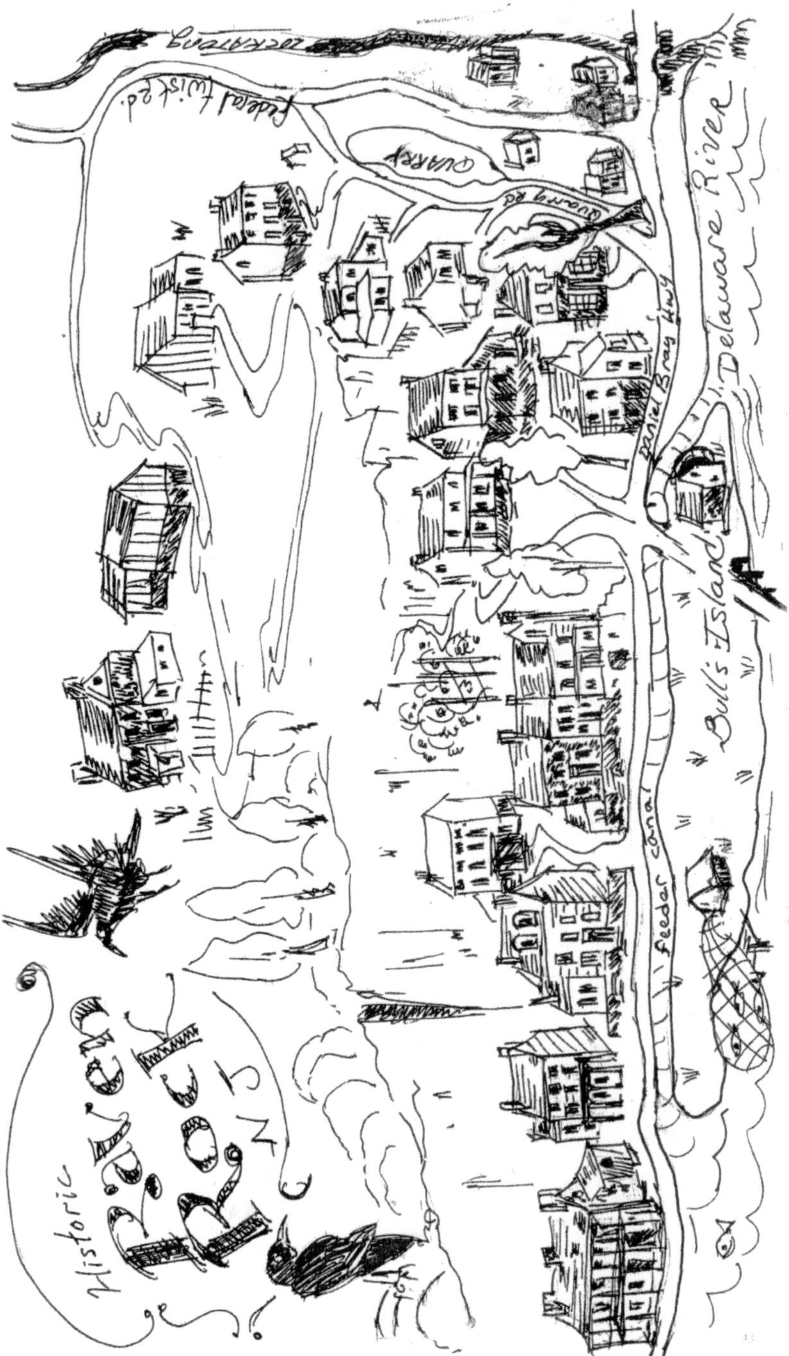

Map drawn by R Curt Chinnici.

These houses were named primarily for their original builders, if known; otherwise, they were named for the owner of record closest to the estimated date of construction. If there is a hyphenated name, it is for a subsequent owner of some duration or significance. (Researched by Marilyn Cummings.)

ISAIAH QUINBY FARMSTEAD—This is the original three-hundred-acre farm, including the land that is now Raven Rock, established by the Isaiah and Rachel Quinby family in 1743.

SAXTONVILLE TAVERN—Named for Nathaniel Saxton, one of the primary owners of Raven Rock property in the early 1800s, though it was not a tavern during his ownership.

LAKE-COLLIGAN HOUSE—Jonas Lake was an early merchant in the area. The Colligan family owned the famous Colligan Inn in Stockton (now the Stockton Inn).

HUNT-READING-SORBY HOUSE—The Jacob and Phillip Hunt families were longtime owners. Captain Richard Reading was a well-known New Jersey senator in the later 1800s. Berthold Sorby was a writer in the mid-1900s.

HEATH-UPDEGROVE HOUSE—The Elijah Heath family owned two adjacent properties. The Updegroves were residents of this house for much of the twentieth century.

SAXTON-HEATH HOUSE—Nathaniel Saxton owned this property and may have resided here for a time.

HEATH-HUFFMAN STORE—Elijah Heath and family were longtime owners of the house complex, which later included a general store and a post office. Mahlon Huffman managed both during the mid-1800s.

WILLIAMSON HOUSE—William Williamson was identified as a shoemaker in the 1870s.

JOHNSON-FEENEY HOUSE—This house may date from as early as the ownership of Wesley Johnson, an early postmaster, and certainly from the ownership of William and Ellen Feeney.

OPDYKE HOUSE—William and James Opdyke were the owners through much of the 1800s; one or both were blacksmiths.

JOHNSON STORE—This building is shown as the C.S. Johnson Store in the 1873 *Beers Atlas*. At various times, it was also a post office and perhaps a tavern.

MCALONE HOUSE—Over time, the extended Joseph McAlone family owned various properties in the village, including Saxtonville Tavern.

DILTS TENANT COTTAGE—Peter Dilts (shown as "Dils" on earlier records) was probably the owner when this small house was built.

RODMAN-LASZLO FARMSTEAD—Joseph Rodman had the only farm actually located in the village. George and Edna Laszlo and their family were owners for several decades in the mid-1900s.

JOHNSON TENANT HOUSE—This house was a part of the Martin Johnson farm until fairly recent times.

VANCAMP-JOHNSON-SCHUCK FARMSTEAD—Guisbert VanCamp was the original owner of this land and very possibly the builder of the earliest part of this house. Martin Johnson and family were the owners for the better part of two centuries. In the later 1900s, it was owned by Anton and Bertha Schuck.

JOHNSON-EMMONS FARMSTEAD—The extended George Johnson family, including the related Emmonses, were owners of this farm for more than a century.

HANKINSON-HUFFMAN FARMSTEAD—The Joseph Hankinson family were eighteenth-century owners. Then the farm was held in the extended family of John Huffman for more than a century.

island and surrounding lands. They, in turn, sold or rented parcels to the first settlers. These settlers were the workers who came to harvest timber, prospect for minerals and clear the land for farming.

On the island, the Snapjaw Fishery used seine nets to catch the abundant sturgeon and shad in the Delaware River. This practice continued into the 1800s, when pollution from industrialization upriver nearly made many species of native fish disappear. In 1780, a distillery was the first commercial building constructed on the island, followed by a water mill in 1794. Mahlon Cooper bought the rights to dam "Bools Creek" to build a grist- and sawmill, a prerequisite for bread-making and for building materials. The mill only lasted until 1823, but the dam remained as a causeway to give access to the island.

Harvesting timber was a huge enterprise, too. The whole eastern seaboard was eventually denuded of trees needed for shipbuilding and construction. Great rafts of logs were steered past the island on their way to Trenton and Philadelphia.

In the 1790s, the main access to Raven Rock was the dirt track of Quarry Road. At the bottom of the hill was a millpond, a distillery and some little houses. The track divided here. Going straight led to the mill and the island. A curve to the right led one north in front of the houses that were built hard against a cliff. The track continued on to Saxtonville Tavern. A small track heading south was a shortcut to Johnson's Ferry. This ferry, at the foot of Federal Twist Road, was the only other way to get to and from the village now called Raven Rock. In their crossing to Lumberville, Pennsylvania, ferry passengers would be exposed to the weather, droughts and floods of the temperamental Delaware River.

If one studies the geography of the newly formed colony of New Jersey and locates the area that is the west-central part of that colony, one comes to the conclusion that the word "remote" fairly accurately describes the Raven Rock environs at the beginning of the 1700s. And if a sojourner planned to traverse the area in question, it becomes immediately obvious that the easiest way to get to this little village from anywhere was by way of the Delaware River. The Lenapes knew this, of course, and without doubt the new settlers came to this realization rather quickly. However, it also became apparent to them that because the river was mighty, treacherous and unpredictable, they needed alternate ways to access this charming outpost.

Most early roads here and elsewhere in the region started as Indian trails. The Lenapes undoubtedly had a well-worn path along the river that later travelers utilized to reach the area. Then, in the 1700s, a road of some significance started developing from the pivotal village of Ringoes, located quite literally at the crossroads of the two most dominant Indian trails in the west-central part of the state—eventually called the Trenton-Easton Turnpike (now Route 579) and Old York Road (now Route 179). That extension took the road west from Ringoes to connect the area on either side of what is now Sergeantsville (at that point, a relatively small dot on early maps between two important mill complexes). Then it was continued to what became Rosemont (also a very small dot) and, by the mid-1700s, from there to Raven Rock—unfortunately by way of a very treacherous path down from the cliffs that the locals later called Democrat Hill.

Ultimately renamed, though not particularly improved, it became today's Quarry Road. The only alternative path down to the little valley was one slightly farther to the north called Stompf Tavern Road, named for a public house situated at the top of that trail. To this day, that option is still a steep, unpaved road that is continually set awry by heavy rainfall. It certainly would not have been a good choice in the 1700s.

In the later eighteenth century, the need to go from the more interior reaches of this area down to a river crossing spurred the improvement of what was then called the road from Milltown (in Kingwood Township) to Painter's Ferry (at Raven Rock), or simply "Ferry Road." This was a slightly easier route to traverse than the ones down Democrat Hill or Stompf Tavern. With its much greater length to reach the top of the cliffs, it therefore was a more gradual incline up from the river. And the purposeful V-shaped switchback (or "the Twist" as locals called it) at the steepest part of the hill allowed the horses and wagons (and cars and trucks later) a resting point on the journey up or down. The road was later named Federal Twist for that reason. In the early twentieth century, that innovation, which was a boon to travelers for so long, was bypassed and the road straightened. (The remains of that area can still be seen on the west side of the road if one searches for it.) Today, then, although still called by that name, both its meaning and its purpose have been lost to time.

In 1853, following the lead of the towns of Stockton and Lambertville, a bridge was constructed from the island across the Delaware to

Lumberville, Pennsylvania. Hence, the ferry service was no longer needed. At last, trade could be done with Pennsylvania. Now it was possible to get to a church or to work safely. The island was still an isolated place, although it was becoming less so.

Until the development of the canals, haulage in the thirteen colonies was limited to navigable rivers and large horse-drawn wagons that used the rutted roads. A canal on the Pennsylvania side of the river was a recent addition, bringing coal down from Lehigh Coal fields to heat the homes of Philadelphia.

In 1830, work started on a canal for the New Jersey side of the river. Upon its completion in 1834, the canal ran from New Brunswick to Trenton and up the Delaware to Bull's Island. The canal section from Trenton up to Bull's Island was mainly a water supply to work the locks. Barges came up to Lambertville, but rarely up to Bull's Island. A lock was built right where the mill once stood; the stones were reused. This lock allowed barge access into the Delaware for dredging and repair work. The lock was cut through the old milldam and causeway to the island to form the top gates. The lower gates were sixty feet downstream. The new lock removed all traces of the old gristmill. A small bridge was built over the top gates to span Bools Creek for access to the island.

Armies of mostly Irish ditch diggers, carpenters and stonemasons toiled from dawn to dusk to construct the new canal. Sadly, there were many worker deaths due to injuries and sickness. An outbreak of cholera took even more lives. It is believed that these men were buried along the canal. Today a stone monument memorial can be found at the park office entrance. A portion of the inscription reads, "May they rest in peace for ever. In memory of those who lost their lives during the construction of the Delaware and Raritan canal." The stone was taken from Lock 13 in New Brunswick. With all the canal construction activity, Raven Rock, in addition to its handful of small houses, now had a general store, a post office, a blacksmith shop, a shoe repair business and a basket factory.

The coming of the railways gradually reduced the need for the canal. Operations continued until the closing of the canal in 1933. The canal, then owned by the Pennsylvania Railroad, relinquished its 933-year lease to the State of New Jersey for the sum of one dollar. The State of New Jersey was puzzled over what to do with this albatross. It came up with a very good idea, which was to use the canal as a water supply to the factories along the canal that needed large amounts of water. The waterway was now a water conduit, earning the state $1.5 million per year. In 1946, the Bull's Island lock was dismantled and replaced by a concrete sluice gate structure for water control. This structure, with the bridge built over it, is what can be seen today. Remnants of the old lock are still visible together with two interesting stone arched water tunnels used for the original canal feed water supply.

In 1854, the Belvidere & Delaware Railroad completed construction of a railway from Trenton to Belvidere for passengers and freight. This was a time of great change all across the United States. Stagecoaches had been replaced by rail service across the entire country by 1867. The limited loads that could be pulled by barge or horse were replaced with the large capacity of the railroads. Manufacturing was replacing agriculture as the primary activity of the nation. Raven Rock had its own station right at the entrance to Bull's Island. Residents could now board the train to Trenton and then go on to New York or Philadelphia. The only enterprises now left in Raven Rock were the store, the basket factory and stone quarry. This quarry had its own rail spur to freight out its popular brownstone. Quarry operations continued until the 1950s. The railroad promoted excursions for its passengers, and Bull's Island was a popular destination. Being an island, it was an exciting place for town dwellers to visit and explore.

Change continued in Raven Rock. The population peaked at about 150 in 1900. On the island, there were then a few residential homes, a gun club and, later, a private campground. As time progressed, less and less happened at Raven Rock, and the little community, with its dreadful gravel track of a road from Stockton, returned to a sleepy backwater. The Great Depression left its mark, causing the closing of the store and post office. Population dropped to about 40.

Just as the railroads superseded the canals, the advent of the automobile brought fierce competition for the railroad. Ridership dwindled, and passenger rail service ended in 1964. Freight continued until 1974, after which the tracks were torn up for scrap.

In 1974, the old canal, now a water conduit, was turned into the Delaware and Raritan (D&R) State Park. This linear park runs from Bull's Island to New Brunswick, New Jersey. The northern end of Bull's Island was upgraded from a private campground to a state-managed

Aerial photo of Raven Rock, New Jersey, and the Delaware River in 1945. The highway from Stockton can be seen on the left where it turns and joins the Missing Link, which is the road that travels past many of the houses in Raven Rock. The Bel-Del train line parallels the road and Bull's Creek. Bull's Island is in the center with the baseball diamond on it. The Raven Rock–Lumberville covered bridge has one section replaced by an iron truss section. Lumberville, Pennsylvania, is the small town on the other side of the bridge. *Collection of Jeffrey Adams.*

camping facility. The little camp office and one residence remained. The new park included a campground, a boat launch area and picnic grounds. The southern part of the island was kept in a natural state to provide habitat for many rare bird species. The park was popular for recreation and was a good example of how the entire Delaware Valley had changed from small working towns in the 1950s to towns dependent on recreation and tourism.

In 1980, with good planning and fortune, the empty railroad right-of-way was added to the Delaware and Raritan State Park. It was converted into a bike path and walking trail. This trail is now one of the biggest attractions in Bull's Island. Linked by the pedestrian bridge over the Delaware to the linear park along the old Pennsylvania canal, Bull's Island has become the ideal starting point for many recreational activities.

What was a rutted gravel road was improved over time to become the road we know today, Route 29. It was completed in 1960, and its completion changed Raven Rock from a small, isolated village into a mere cluster of houses on a busy road. Population now is just thirty-five people. Upward of one thousand drivers per day speed through Raven Rock, their minds intent on their destination and totally unaware of the changes the road has brought.

A small relief to truck traffic on the highway came in 1996 when Route 29 was designated a Scenic Byway. Heavy, nonlocal carriers were banned.

The island, once remote and uninhabited, is now a place of recreation, and on weekends, the island fills with people enjoying picnicking, fishing, biking, boating and walking. The Delaware River, while tranquil most of the time, occasionally shows its darker side. Heavy flooding seemed to happen roughly four times in a period of one hundred years. There were extremely damaging floods in 1903, in 1936 and, the biggest of all, in 1955.

Then there was a stretch of fifty years—long enough to think that with all the major Delaware River tributaries dammed and controlled, flooding was a thing of the past. Three consecutive floods between 2004 and 2006 were a severe rebuttal to this idea. There was extensive damage to the campground, which was quickly repaired. On the island, the D&R Park Commission added a fine new park office, modern showers, bathrooms in the campground and good paved lanes to the campsites. After each flood, the new office flooded but was easily repairable. The bathrooms, roads and campsites, though, suffered heavy damage due to their lower elevation.

However, with the campground in good order, there came another calamity in the spring of 2011. An enormous sycamore tree fell and killed a man who was camping. Severe internal rotting of the tree's lateral roots caused it to fall. Since the campground had many more sycamore trees, camping was suspended for the season. That same year, in September, Hurricane Irene arrived, producing yet another flood. Restrooms and roads were once again damaged. Shortly after this flood, a freak early snowstorm brought down many huge trees. The entire campground was littered with fallen trees and heavy limbs.

The final blow for the campground came in the form of a lawsuit against the state as a result of the earlier tragic, fatal accident. As of this

The Saint Patrick's Day flood of 1936. Local residents navigate the floodwaters by rowboat. The millpond lies under the water just behind them, yet the Bel-Del train tracks are still above water. *Courtesy of Luverne Updegrove Caulton.*

writing, the state has decided to end camping on the island indefinitely. On the advice of tree experts, the state is reviewing the felling of all the sycamore trees and replanting the area with trees more suited to flooding conditions. Not all people are convinced that removal of the sycamores is necessary, and the issue is being contested. Today, the park is essentially the center of all that happens in Raven Rock. At this point in time, the future of the park is essentially the future of Raven Rock.

Raven Rock at the Beginning

Marfy Goodspeed

Raven Rock has had several names. It was once known as Saxtonville (also as Saxtons Ville or Sextonville) before reverting back to Raven Rock. But even before it was Raven Rock, it had a Lenape name.

The earliest documented notice of the place came in 1708, when the township of Amwell was created by the New Jersey state legislature. The boundary description began "at a place called Mauanissing." This was the point on the Delaware River where the dividing line between today's Kingwood and Delaware townships begins, just north of Raven Rock. Mauanissing is obviously a Lenape name, but the meaning of the name is obscure. The first time the name "Raven Rock" appears in documents is in the will of John Ladd in 1731, a very early date, when European settlement in the area had hardly begun. It suggests that "Raven Rock" might be a translation of the Lenape's "Mauanissing."

With a name as poetic as Raven Rock, many theories have been suggested for its origin. Egbert T. Bush, a Hunterdon historian writing in the 1930s, thought it might be a corruption of "riven rock," which aptly describes "the great rock which is the distinguishing figure of the village." As you approach the cliff, Bush wrote, the "perpendicular rock…seems to become overhanging…There it stands from 90 to 100 feet high, with a dwelling house so close that it appears to be at its foot." That house is now known as the Saxtonville Tavern.

Some have written that the name "Raven Rock" is derived from hawks that were observed riding the thermal air currents to rise up the cliff face. But hawks and ravens are very different birds. Perhaps at one time ravens were seen circling around at the top of the cliff. This may be true if the name originated with the Lenapes. But if it was a European name, then "Raven" could refer to the color of the rock.

A former resident and local historian, B.A. Sorby, had his own version. Sorby wrote several articles on the Raven Rock neighborhood in 1959 when the State of New Jersey was building the "missing link" of Route 29 from Raven Rock to Byram. Sorby wrote that red shale and sandstone were blasted away near Byram to make way for the road and that the site was "located a short distance from New Jersey's 'Great Stone Face' which towers over the river at this point from the rock which gives the village its name."

Although the "Great Stone Face" probably did "give the village its name," it should be noted that the "Stone Face" was made of argillite, not red shale and sandstone. It is the tip of the Hunterdon Plateau, a massive outcropping of sedimentary rock that resists erosion, unlike sandstone and shale. Clearly, no one will ever be able to explain the name with absolute certainty.

Bull's Island is another ancient neighborhood name, frequently written in old documents as "Bool's Island." It was originally known as Ponnacussing or Paunacussing. This was probably a European guess at the real Lenape name, which is supposed to mean "place where the powder was given us." This seems so unlikely that it must have been someone's fantasy of Lenape history.

The name "Bull's Island" likely comes from an early surveyor, Richard Bull of Gloucester County (circa 1675–circa 1722), who made many surveys in early Amwell Township on behalf of the West Jersey proprietors. Most of his surveys date back to the time when surveys were first being made in this vicinity, from 1710 to 1720. "Bool" is probably the way his name was pronounced, as it was common for people to write words phonetically in the eighteenth century.

It was Richard Bull who surveyed a 625-acre property on November 11, 1712, for himself and his partner, John Ladd, also of Gloucester. Later, Bull and Ladd decided to divide the property between them, and on February 18, 1721, Richard Bull gave up his rights for half of his tract

The Quinby House, or "old stone mansion," as it was called by local residents. The original house was built in 1743 on three hundred acres. It may have been made of logs and then added onto by later generations. If this late 1800s photo tells the proper tale, the oldest section of the house (back right of photo) appears to be a one-and-a-half-story, one-room structure, probably with a loft and made of stone. *Courtesy of Eva Zdepski Platt.*

to John Ladd, retaining his rights in the remainder. Oddly enough, Bull's Island and the area of Raven Rock went to Ladd rather than to Bull.

Even though the name "Raven Rock" was in use by 1731, it was not always the preferred name. When Moses Quinby advertised for return of a stray horse in 1794, he identified himself as "living at a noted place called Bull's Island in Amwell Township, Hunterdon County." But Quinby was not living on the island; his home was in the village of Raven Rock, before it was a village.

John Ladd was one of the Quaker immigrants who came to west New Jersey in 1678. He was also on hand when William Penn was designing the layout of his new town of Philadelphia. Family tradition notes that Penn offered Ladd a choice of one of the best squares in the city or thirty pounds; Ladd chose the money, whereupon Penn is supposed to have said, "John thou art a ladd by name and a lad by nature, doesn't thee know that Philadelphia will be a great city?" Penn, of course, was right.

Apparently, John Ladd managed to prosper anyway, for he died a wealthy man in about 1740 in Deptford, Gloucester, New Jersey, with hundreds of acres to leave to his three surviving children. Ladd's will

F. Hammond's map shows the Bull and Ladd tract and also the property that was sold to Joseph Reading in 1773. That was the land originally allotted to Richard Bull in 1721. Hammond did not include Isaiah Quinby, east of Joseph Reading. The dotted line indicated the division between Kingwood and Amwell Townships. *Courtesy of Goodspeedhistories.com.*

of 1731 left to his daughter, Catharine, the three hundred acres called Raven Rock above the falls on or near the Delaware River in Amwell Township. This gift included the entirety of Bull's Island. Catharine (or "Katherine") Ladd married John Howell in 1734. They had no interest in taking up residence on the Raven Rock plantation, and in 1743, Catharine Ladd Howell sold the property to Isaiah Quinby.

A map created by D. Stanton Hammond of the early proprietary tracts in Hunterdon County shows the Bull and Ladd tract, as well as a part in Kingwood Township that was sold to Joseph Reading in 1773. That was the land originally allotted to Richard Bull in 1721. Hammond's map does not show Isaiah Quinby to the east of Joseph Reading, but it seems to indicate that Raven Rock was on the property of Peter Fretwell when, in fact, it belongs in the unidentified tract that was purchased by Isaiah Quinby—between Fretwell and Reading.

ISAIAH QUINBY

Isaiah Quinby (1716–1807) was the youngest of the eleven children of Josiah Quinby and Mary Mullineaux of New York. In 1743, at the age of twenty-seven, he married Rachel Warford (1725–1777) of Kingwood Township a few months before his purchase of the Ladd property. Rachel was the daughter of John Warford and Elizabeth Stout, who came from Monmouth County to Hunterdon in 1729. At the time of his marriage, Isaiah Quinby was probably working on his father-in-law's plantation or perhaps for his older brother Ephraim Quinby (1700–1767), who purchased land in Amwell Township as early as 1727. At that time, Amwell Township included all of present-day Delaware, Raritan and East and West Amwell, as well as Stockton and Lambertville and even parts of Readington Township.

Isaiah Quinby had many ways of exploiting the location of his newly acquired plantation. He was a prosperous farmer, but he also had a sixty-acre island along the Delaware River, an ideal location for catching the shad and sturgeon that migrated upriver. Quinby also was able to ship produce and timber downriver to Trenton and Philadelphia, and it is possible that he set up a mill on one of the creeks flowing into the river across from the island.

Two years after buying Ladd's 300 acres, Quinby bought a 10-acre lot from his neighbor, Marmaduke Leet, for nine pounds. This land was part of the 650 acres owned by Peter Fretwell in 1711, located between the Mount Amwell tract of John Reading and the tract surveyed to John Ladd and Richard Bull. Perhaps Quinby wanted this triangle of land because it contained the lower part of today's Quarry Road, where an early road ran from Raven Rock to Prallsville. The lot did not go far enough to include the quarry itself, but it may have included a run of water that would be useful for a mill along the creek that divided Raven Rock from Bull's Island.

DURING THE REVOLUTION

Very little activity took place at Raven Rock during the Revolution. When Washington took his army across the Delaware in 1776, he might have made use of boats that were borrowed from Bull's Island residents, but Daniel Bray and his men did not use the island to conceal the boats.

In 1777, while the British were still in New Jersey, Isaiah Quinby's wife, Rachel, died at age fifty-one, after raising thirteen children. Only one of them died in childhood. The youngest child was Job, born in 1768. Isaiah Quinby married again only a year after Rachel died. His second wife, Hannah Kinsey, was also a Quaker; they married at Buckingham Friends Meeting.

There is no evidence that the sons of Isaiah and Rachel Quinby served in the local militia or the Continental army. The explanation is that this was a Quaker family who worshiped at the Buckingham Friends Meeting House in Bucks County, Pennsylvania, and as Quakers, they would have abstained from participating in any military actions.

Quinby's sons all married women from Bucks County. Aaron and Moses Quinby both married in 1782. Aaron, born 1757, married Lydia Balderston and took up residence in Bucks County. Moses (1759–1824) married Jane Fell, daughter of John Fell of Warwick, Pennsylvania. He married again in 1801, to Hannah Good. The third son, James, born 1765, married Margaret Good (sister of Hannah) in 1803. He was too young to fight in the Revolution, as was son Job, born in 1768, who married Martha Cadwallader.

At the conclusion of the Revolutionary War, Reading (or "Redding") Howell prepared a map of the Delaware River area for the new governments of Pennsylvania and New Jersey. It was dated December 3, 1785, and was intended to assist the states in setting their boundary along the river. On the Pennsylvania side, opposite Bull's Island, was the "Hon. G. Wall's Saw Mill & Plantation." Across the river in New Jersey was "Quimby's" at the tavern site—just the name and a symbol for a house. There was no indication that a tavern or a mill existed there.

The location of the "Quimby" name near Bull's Creek does not refer to Isaiah Quinby, who had set up his homestead up the hill, accessible today by Federal Twist Road. The separate habitation for "Quimby" by the river was undoubtedly the stone house owned by Moses Quinby. B.A. Sorby was convinced that a tavern was located there as early as 1782, but I have found no record to support such an early date. Moses Quinby was married in 1782 and beginning a family. The Quinby genealogy recites that after marrying Hannah Good in 1801, Moses Quinby took his new wife "to live in the little house" at the foot of the large split rock along the

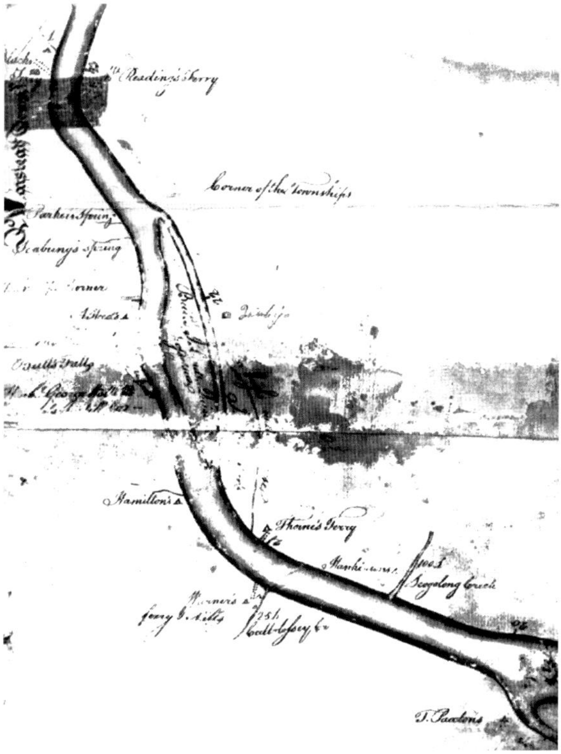

Reading Howell's map of 1785. This map shows early land ownership and ferry locations. Bull's Island and the creek alongside it are also drawn on the map. Moses Quinby, the earliest resident of Raven Rock, is indicated, and so is George Wall, who established Lumberville, Pennsylvania. *Courtesy of Goodspeedhistories.com and Edna Laszlo.*

Hunt-Reading-Sorby House stereoview image. These popular stereoview cards had two slightly different images, and when viewed through a lens, the image appeared to be three-dimensional. This card shows one of the earliest houses in Raven Rock, which was the home of Moses Quinby. A large vegetable garden is over what is now the Daniel Bray Highway. *Courtesy of Hunterdon County Historical Society.*

river. Sorby may have thought that the "little house" was also home to Moses's first wife, which is possible; this would make Quinby the earliest known resident of Raven Rock.

BULL'S ISLAND FISHERIES

Fishing rights in the Delaware River were legally transferable, and leases often show up in deeds. Isaiah Quinby is known to have leased fishing rights in the Delaware River on February 30, 1782. He probably did this earlier, but this is the first record available. Quinby gave a lease to Ann Quinby, Moses Quinby, John Woolverton "and others." A second lease was given on March 17, 1786, to Aaron Quinby, Moses Quinby, Isaac Rittenhouse "and others." Quinby also leased a fishery to George Wall of Pennsylvania on the same date, "beginning at the head of Bull's Falls and drawing out near the lower part of the island." Its formal name was the Prime Hope fishery, but it was more generally known by the very descriptive name of "Snapjaw." When the property was sold in 1814, exception was made to allow continued access to the river for work on the Snapjaw fishery. The Snapjaw came into possession of Jabez White in 1811, when he bought it from the heirs of George Wall.

By 1786, Isaiah Quinby had increased his holdings to 460 acres plus 100 acres unimproved. When he was taxed that year, sons Aaron and Moses Quinby were counted as single men. In 1790, Isaiah Quinby was taxed on 255 acres and a fishery, while son Aaron was taxed on 150 acres, son Moses on 180 acres and son Job on 50 acres. This comes to 635 acres, which sounds like the original 625 belonging to Bull and Ladd plus 10 acres from Marmaduke Leet. But that is not the case, since Joseph Reading owned the western portion of the Bull and Ladd tract.

When Isaiah Quinby wrote his will in 1804, he left his fishery known as "Bullcap" to his son James and to daughter Martha Quinby Blackfan. The will did not describe the location of this fishery, but it must have been in the vicinity of Bull's Island. The Bullcap might have been the same fishery that Isaiah Quinby leased on February 20, 1794, to his sons Moses, Aaron and James. This particular fishery is of special interest because of the exceptions in the lease. According to B.A. Sorby, this third lease allowed Mahlon Cooper and Robert Curry the privilege of building a milldam across Bull's Creek on the south side of "Dead Creek," with the idea of directing the waters of Bull's Creek down to Dead Creek, thus improving the working of their mill.

Bull's Creek was the waterway that separated Bull's Island from the rest of Amwell Township. Sorby also wrote that the milldam is gone, now lying beneath the canal lock and the road over the railroad tracks. However, the railroad tracks he referred to are also gone, replaced with the beautiful walking trail along the Delaware & Raritan (D&R) Canal. The fisheries are gone, too, phased out with the coming of the canal and the railroad.

NEW OWNERS OF RAVEN ROCK

As the end of the eighteenth century approached, ownership of Raven Rock and Bull's Island was changed from a single large landowner to multiple owners with different ways of exploiting the resources of the neighborhood.

Mahlon Cooper and Robert Curry were the first people of record to operate a mill at Raven Rock. On October 14, 1799, Isaiah Quinby sold a ten-acre lot on Bull's Creek to Mahlon Cooper for £500. However, the lease of 1794 makes it clear that Cooper and Curry were already acting as partners and had been for five years before purchasing the mill lot.

Probably as a continuation of his plans to dispose of his property, Isaiah Quinby carved out a tract of seventy-five acres adjoining Bull's Island and, on March 24, 1801, sold it along with the island to the most important man on the Pennsylvania side of the river, George Wall, generally credited with being the founder of the town of Lumberville. Wall paid $4,000 for the whole, excepting out the fisheries that had been leased and the rights of Cooper and Curry to build a dam for their mill. The deed identified the stream of water separating the island from the mainland of New Jersey as "Bull's Creek."

Only six days after this deed was signed, George Wall conveyed the seventy-five-acre tract to Isaiah Quinby's son Moses for £700. Mr. Wall made a handsome profit. (In 1800, £1 was equal to $4.77, making £700 equivalent to $3,340.89.) Wall paid $4,000 for the whole tract, but he got nearly that much from Moses Quinby for just seventy-five acres. Given the dates of the two deeds—from Isaiah Quinby to George Wall and from Wall to Moses Quinby—it seems likely that the division (Wall to get the island, Quinby to get the rest) was agreed on beforehand.

Moses Quinby and his first wife, Jane Fell, had eleven children from 1783 to 1799, the year that Jane died. On January 13, 1801, Quinby married his second wife, Hannah Good, daughter of Edward Good and Eleanor Harris of Plumstead, Pennsylvania. Moses and Hannah eventually had seven children, for a total of eighteen children of Moses Quinby, almost all of whom survived to adulthood.

By 1801, Mahlon Cooper and Robert Curry had been operating their mill for seven years. To get more control over the water power for their mill, they purchased the lower half of Bull's Island from George Wall. A mortgage dated May 1, 1801, shows that Cooper and Curry mortgaged the thirty-acre property to Wall, promising to pay $533.33 in two installments. George Wall was primarily interested in the northern half of Bull's Island, which was the location of his Prime Hope/Snapjaw fishery. The fishery began at the northern tip of the island and ran down the riverside nearly its whole length. The mortgage to Wall also shows that after Wall's death, his executors on May 18, 1805, assigned the Cooper-Curry mortgage to Samuel Curry, brother of Robert Curry, and to Nathaniel Shewell, Samuel Curry's brother-in-law.

On May 22, 1804, Isaiah Quinby of Amwell, "being of advanced age" (he was eighty-four years old), wrote his will. He left to his third wife, Miriam (maiden name Betts), £100 and whatever goods she brought with her when they married, along with a riding horse, a cow, a feather bed and bedding and use of the house during her widowhood, plus the yearly interest on £200. The house "where I now live," which sits at the top of Federal Twist hill in Delaware Township, was to be shared with son James, who would inherit the three-hundred-acre plantation after Miriam's death even though he was not the oldest surviving son. Son Moses Quinby did not get any bequest. He was only mentioned as a bordering owner to the three hundred acres left to James Quinby. The fact that Isaiah Quinby made no provision for Moses suggests that the arrangement with Wall to provide Moses with seventy-five acres was considered part of his inheritance.

Isaiah Quinby died on June 6, 1807. His wife, Miriam, survived him until her death on September 20, 1811. She also wrote a will in which she provided for her daughters and for her granddaughters. One of her provisions left the money due her on a bond from son Moses to her granddaughters, the five daughters of Moses Quinby, deducting out moneys due from Miriam Quinby to Moses Quinby.

Just to show how important names were to the people of that time, in another provision of Miriam Quinby's will, she left a clock to her son James if, and only if, he had a son named Isaiah. If that did not happen, then the clock was to go to Aaron Quinby's son Isaiah. It is also an indicator of the Quinby wealth that they actually had a clock. Most Hunterdon families of this time did not.

Miriam named her son James as executor, along with son-in-law John Wolverton and another important person in the history of this neighborhood, Nathaniel Saxton. In fact, it was probably Saxton who drew up Miriam Quinby's will. He was, by this time, an important person in Raven Rock—so important that by 1814, the village name had been changed to Saxtonville (or Saxtonsville).

THE MILL IN RAVEN ROCK

The mill at Saxtonville has a curious history. According to a later deed, the mill lot contained a gristmill, a sawmill and two dwelling houses that were undoubtedly inhabited by the Cooper and Curry families. Today, the ten-acre mill lot is partly covered by Highway 29. Neither of the houses, nor the mill itself, has survived.

Milling was a risky operation in the eighteenth and early nineteenth centuries. Millers were always going into debt, perhaps because their customers bought on credit and were slow to pay. To cover operating expenses, millers themselves had to borrow money. Cooper and Curry had several creditors, the largest being George Holcombe Jr., to whom was owed $6,000.00 (plus interest of $375.16). This was probably a mortgage.

In 1807, the creditors of Cooper and Curry took them to court, which ruled that the sheriff should levy on their goods and chattels to produce the sums needed and, if that was insufficient, to levy on their lands and tenements. Sheriff Nathan Price advertised the sale of two lots in the "Trenton True American." He described them as "30 acres of land on the river Delaware, being part of an island called Bull's Island and also on ten acres of land adjoining Robert Nailor with a gristmill and a sawmill

Floodwaters over the damaged canal bridge at Bull's Island, Saint Patrick's Day 1936. This is the general location of one of the mills that existed along Bull's Creek. *Courtesy of Luverne Updegrove Caulton.*

and two dwelling houses, all in the twp. of Amwell." What was offered for sale on the first Tuesday of March 1808 was the moiety, or one-half interest of Robert Curry in the mill properties. As no acceptable bid was made, the sale was adjourned to March 15, 1808, when the moiety was sold to Nathaniel Saxton for only seven dollars. Cooper's moiety was sold later, on May 1, 1808, to George Holcombe Jr. for only fifty dollars. Saxton had probably persuaded Holcombe to partner with him. Saxton's correspondence suggests that he was the one in charge of the mill, even though Holcombe had more milling experience, having owned the mill at Headquarters since 1793.

Although Mahlon Cooper left Hunterdon shortly after the sheriff's sale, it is possible that he had a son, John Cooper, who remained behind and married Mary Nailor (or "Naylor") on August 22, 1818, at the house of Joseph Rodman in Raven Rock (Saxtonville). Mary might have been the daughter of Robert Naylor, who in 1804 bought part of Moses Quinby's seventy-five acres bordering the mill lot.

Mahlon Cooper probably moved to Pennsylvania and took up construction work. His talents did not go unnoticed. The highly esteemed architect Benjamin Henry Latrobe, who was hired to help construct a house in Washington, D.C., for the years 1815 to 1818, wrote that Cooper and also "S. Ellis…both from Philadelphia [were] perfect masters of their business."

Robert Curry's family came from Pennsylvania. His father, Laughlin Curry, who was born in about 1737, was taxed in Philadelphia as early as 1769 and again in 1774. In about 1760, he married Margaret Barber, daughter of John Barber and Magdalene Johnson of Amwell Township. John Barber named Margaret and her children in his will of 1795. Laughlin Curry died on November 1, 1803, and was buried at the Barber Cemetery, as was his wife, Margaret, who lived on until August 26, 1828.

Laughlin and Margaret Curry had six children, the second son being Robert, who was probably born in about 1765 in Pennsylvania. His sister Margaret married George Lukens on March 1, 1806. The Lukens family of Pennsylvania was connected by marriage with the Quinbys of Raven Rock.

Robert Curry must have left Hunterdon after the sheriff's sale of 1808 and moved back to Pennsylvania. There was a Robert Curry who married Anne Larew on May 5, 1817, in Hunterdon County, but the Robert Curry who was partner of Mahlon Cooper would have been about fifty-two years old by then. The Larew family in Hunterdon County was an extensive one, but I cannot identify this Anne. With so many questions unanswered, we must say farewell to the elusive Cooper and Curry, millers of Raven Rock.

THE LAST OF THE QUINBYS

Moses Quinby began selling small lots out of his seventy-five acres at Raven Rock in 1804, keeping a lot of sixteen acres, where he lived with his family until 1815. Quinby acquired and sold other properties nearby, but it is the seventy-five-acre tract that is most important, since the entire village of Raven Rock is situated there. It included the triangular ten-acre lot sold by Marmaduke Leet to Moses Quinby's father, Isaiah.

On June 12, 1804, only three years after the seventy-five acres were acquired, Moses Quinby, yeoman of Amwell, and wife Hannah sold nineteen acres and thirty-three perches to Benjamin Longstreath, millwright of Amwell, for £350. This lot ran from Bull's Creek back up a large hollow in the cliff to a line bordering the farm of Isaiah Quinby. As a millwright, Longstreath probably did some work for millers Cooper and Curry. A millwright was a carpenter and a mechanic who could set

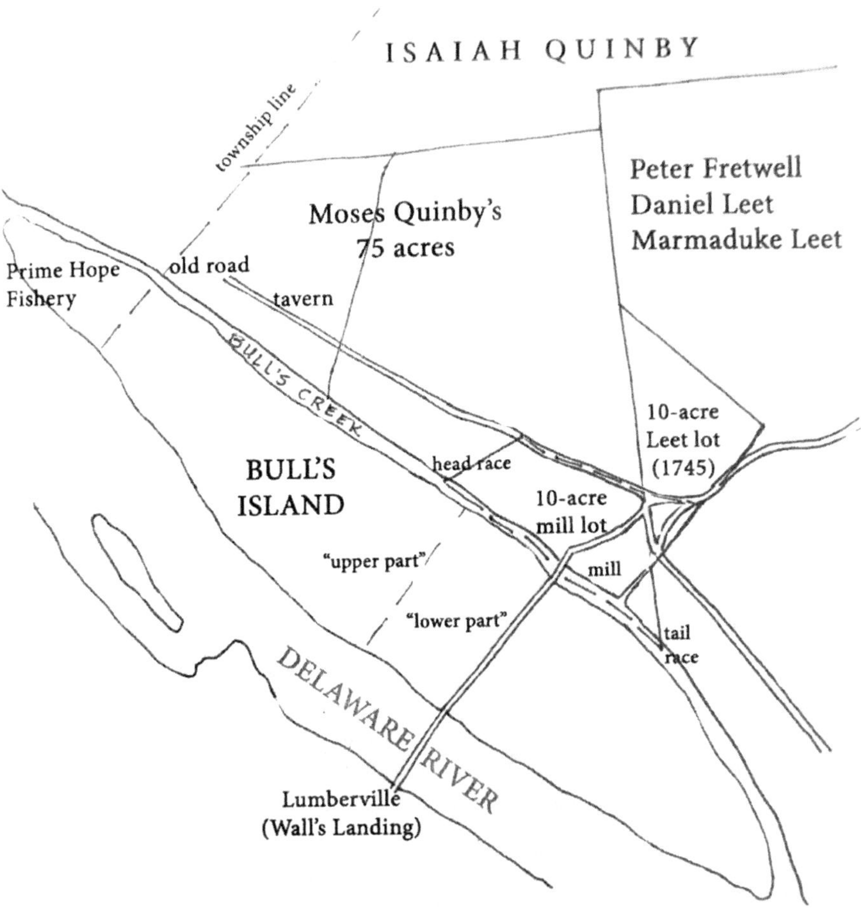

Bull's Island and Raven Rock in 1801. The village of Raven Rock was entirely situated in the seventy-five acres held by Moses Quinby. Also seen is the mill lot, which was in operation by 1794. The "tavern" did not come into use until 1833. Also shown is the Prime Hope fishery, which came into operation as early as 1786. *Courtesy of Goodspeedhistories.com.*

up and repair the drive shafts, gears and belts needed for any kind of mill, be it a sawmill, flour mill, linseed oil mill, plaster mill or clover seed mill. In Hunterdon County, millwrights also built the huge wheels that powered those mills. Longstreath did not stay long; on May 1, 1806, he and wife Isabella sold the lot on Bull's Creek to Jacob Hunt for $1,166.67 ($61.00 per acre). This was about $500.00 less than Longstreath had paid Moses Quinby. Jacob Hunt, in turn, divided the nineteen acres into smaller lots facing the creek.

On August 27, 1804, Moses Quinby, yeoman of Amwell, and wife Hannah sold a forty-acre parcel just east of the Longstreath lot, bordering the mill lot. The purchaser was Robert Naylor, also yeoman of Amwell, who paid £4,000, or £100 ($477) per acre, an extravagant price. Just like Benjamin Longstreath's lot, the Naylor lot included what is now frontage along Highway 29, as well as land up on the plateau. Access to this back land could only be from the triangular ten-acre lot that fronts on today's Quarry Road, which may explain why Isaiah Quinby bought it in 1745 but does not explain why the forty acres was so expensive.

Little is known of Robert Naylor; he was likely an English immigrant who bought and sold properties in the Raven Rock area from the late 1700s through 1820. He wrote his will on December 20, 1827, leaving only ten dollars to his wife, Mary, and fifty cents to each of his children: Mary, Robert, John, David, Jane and Sarah. All his real estate was left to his son Robert Jr.

After selling forty acres to Naylor and nineteen acres to Longstreath, Moses Quinby was left with sixteen acres, more or less. This was the location of the future Saxtonville Tavern, as well as where Quinby lived and kept his store. Moses and Hannah Quinby seem to have divided their time between Raven Rock and Plumstead in Bucks County, where they were living in 1807. But by 1809, they were once again in Amwell Township when Moses Quinby sold the last of his Amwell properties. On June 3, 1809, he signed a "Memorandum of Agreement" between himself and Nathaniel Saxton in which Quinby agreed to sell to Saxton for $400 all that lot in Amwell on that part of the Delaware called Bull's Creek adjoining lands of Baker Phillips, James Quinby and Jacob Hunt of fifteen to seventeen acres, being the residue of lands owned by said Quinby at that place. Saxton was to pay $200 to cancel the mortgage owned by Mrs. Miriam Quinby, as well as the remainder in two installments of $100 each, in 1810 and 1811.

According to the Quinby genealogy, Moses Quinby was not suited for storekeeping, which is a nice way of saying that Quinby could not stay out of debt. Fortunately, Nathaniel Saxton gave him a way out. But Saxton drove a much harder bargain than Benjamin Longstreath did, paying only about twenty-five dollars per acre, while Longstreath paid the equivalent of eighty-seven dollars per acre. The transaction was finalized in 1810 when a deed was signed on March 28.

Moses Quinby moved his family to Buckingham for a time, but in 1813, he received a certificate from the Buckingham Monthly Meeting dismissing him and his family from the Falls Township Meeting. The Quinby genealogy speculates that he also resided in Upper Makefield Township, Pennsylvania. By 1816, he and his family had moved to Wrightstown and joined the monthly meeting there. Although life was a struggle for Moses Quinby, his son, Dr. John Quinby, prospered. John moved to the vicinity of Wilmington, Delaware, and bought a farm there for his father's retirement. Moses Quinby died near New Castle on November 1, 1824, at age sixty-five. On June 22, 1832, his widow, Hannah died at age sixty-two.

Although there were no more Quinbys at Raven Rock, James Quinby, brother of Moses, was still living at the old farm up the hill on Federal Twist Road. James Quinby died in 1830, leaving his farm to his sons. But his estate was encumbered by debts, so the land was sold to satisfy creditors. The Quinby children all moved west, bringing the Quinby era to an end.

Saxtonville

Marfy Goodspeed

More than anyone else, Nathaniel Saxton created the village of Raven Rock, although for him the name was Saxtonville. Saxton became a widely respected attorney, a member of the state senate and a chancery court reporter. But when he made his first investments in Raven Rock and Bull's Island, he was just beginning his career in law and real estate.

Saxton was born in Hopewell Township in about 1775 to Charles Saxton and Elizabeth Pelton. He came to Flemington in about 1800 to study law under Lucius W. Stockton, the Hunterdon County clerk, and his successor, Ralph Hunt. He was not admitted to the bar until he was thirty years old, in 1804. For the next thirty years, he practiced law in Flemington, except for a term as reporter for the court of chancery in Trenton. He was described as "a man of sound legal learning and of varied literacy and scientific acquirements" and as "the artificer of his fame and fortune."

The first time that Nathaniel Saxton bought property for a long-term investment was in 1808, as one of two purchasers of the Cooper-Curry mill lot in Raven Rock. He bought his share on March 15 for $7, while George Holcombe, who had given Cooper and Curry their $6,000 mortgage, bought the other share for $50.

Saxton was the active manager of the Raven Rock mill. In the summer of 1809, he wrote to his father, Charles Saxton, in Shamokin, Pennsylvania, asking him for help. His father responded, "A few lines From you…Informed us that…you had purchased Mills on the Delaware and that you wisht

Saxton-Heath House and Heath-Huffman House and Store, a most charming group of houses in the area. They were built in stages, with the stone section being built circa 1800. The section on the right, circa 1830, was built as a store. The middle wooden section joined both houses. The dormer on the upper right had a hoist to lift supplies to an attic storage area. The summer kitchen on the far left completes this classic and early assemblage. Successive owners of any duration were Jacob Hunt in 1806, Nathaniel Saxton in 1810 and Peter Dilts from 1819 to 1839. The house then came into the Elijah Heath family from 1839 to 1867 and was where renter Mahlon Huffman operated a general store and post office through the mid-1800s. *Photo by R. Curt Chinnici.*

either Nais [Ananais] or my self to come Down and assist in taking care of them…I rather think one of us could come Next spring." Eventually, it was Saxton's brother, Ananais Saxton, who came to help with the mills, but there is little record of his presence here. Saxton shipped his lumber on rafts down the Delaware River to Philadelphia, where his agent, Albertus King, arranged for their sale. King advised Saxton on what types of wood were most in demand, like boards sawn to five-eighths of an inch in thickness.

THE BRIDGE AT BULL'S ISLAND

Up until this time, the only way to get across the river was by ferry. There were several ferries between Coryell's Ferry (Lambertville) and Alexandria, later known as Frenchtown. The ferry closest to Bull's Island was run by Martin Johnson, who had succeeded Jacob Painter. It was located near the point where Federal Twist Road intersects with Highway 29. All evidence of it has been erased.

In 1806, two of the Delaware River ferries were replaced by bridges, one at Easton and one at Trenton. Their advantages were immediately obvious. A bridge avoided the biggest problem associated with ferries: it could be crossed in almost any kind of weather. Ferries could not run during spring freshets, when the river was frozen over or in the summer when the water level dropped too low. Occasionally, travelers could simply ride their horses across the river, but often they could not and would have to wait in a nearby tavern for conditions to improve. Bridges, especially sturdy covered bridges, were the answer. Private companies, which raised funds for construction by selling shares, built them. The profits, which went toward bridge maintenance and to shareholder dividends, came from the tolls they charged.

For Nathaniel Saxton, it was obvious that there should be a bridge at Bull's Island. In 1810, he printed a petition to the legislatures of New Jersey and Pennsylvania and began collecting signatures. But supporters of a bridge at Howell's or Mitchell's Ferry (Stockton) and Coryell's Ferry (Lambertville) had already submitted petitions to the legislatures.

In composing his petition, Saxton explained why Bull's Island was a superior location. He noted that the river at Bull's Island was far narrower than it was at other locations, making it ideal for a crossing, and that

The Johnson Ferry House, demolished in 1959 to make way for the Daniel Bray Highway. It was originally owned by Martin Johnson and later his son, William Johnson, who closed the ferry sometime after 1814. *Courtesy of Goodspeedhistories.com.*

Bull's Island was "the most central, and on this account the most eligible place." Saxton had no trouble getting signatures. There were hundreds, from Hunterdon, Morris and Sussex Counties (Warren was still part of Sussex), as well as from residents of Solebury and Buckingham Townships in Bucks County.

The legislatures of New Jersey and Pennsylvania gradually came to a consensus on the location of a bridge. By September 1811, the decision had been made. Commissioners appointed by the two state legislatures determined that Mitchell's Ferry was the best location. Patent letters of incorporation for a new bridge company were issued in New Jersey on August 17, 1812, signed by Governor Joseph Bloomfield, and in Pennsylvania on September 1.

Eventually, Saxton's bridge did get built, but not until after the Delaware & Raritan Canal had opened in 1834, which made a bridge at Bull's Island a necessity. The Lumberville–Bull's Island Bridge was opened in 1856.

DEVELOPING SAXTONVILLE

After setting up his milling operation in 1809, Saxton began to acquire other properties in Raven Rock. He arranged with Moses Quinby to buy the house and fifteen-acre lot where Quinby was living, later known as the Saxtonville Tavern. Saxton probably rented out the house while he maintained his residence in Flemington, where he carried on his legal practice in partnership with George C. Maxwell.

Like the mill, Saxton probably found someone to take over the store that Moses Quinby had run in the house, but he probably never ran a tavern there. When reference to a tavern or inn was made in advertisements, the common expression was "at the house of…," but there was never such a mention of the house of N. Saxton in Saxtonville nor at the house of anyone else in Saxtonville or Bull's Island until Richard Bennett in 1833.

Next, Saxton bought up the remainder of Moses Quinby's land, the 40.00 acres Quinby sold to Robert Nailor (or Naylor), now reduced to 37.25 acres, which ran from today's Quarry Road northwest to encompass the farm that later on was owned by George and Edna Lazlo. Saxton also purchased some of the small lots created by Jacob Hunt.

Saxton's largest acquisition took place in December 1812 when he bought the northern half of Bull's Island. Previously, the island had been divided in half, with the southern half sold to Cooper and Curry and later acquired by Saxton and Holcombe. The rest of the island remained with George Wall until his death, when his heirs sold it to the brothers Joseph and Jonathan Townsend of Solebury. They sold the upper half of the island to Nathaniel Saxton for about fifty-eight dollars per acre, a very high price. This deed excepted out the right of the heirs of George Wall to have access the river side of the island to maintain the Prime Hope/Snapjaw fishery, which was located at the northern end of the island. Saxton now owned the whole of the island and a half share of the mill lot, along with the Naylor tract, which amounted to most of the real estate in Raven Rock.

Land records show that the first mention of Saxtonville is on a deed dated July 1, 1814, when Nathaniel Saxton sold his half share in the mill lot to George Holcombe, owner of the other half. In a mortgage of that year, the place was called "Saxton Ville." Another early reference to Saxtonville was found in an 1818 road petition near "Saxton Vill." As for the author of the name, it was most likely Saxton himself, since the name was most frequently used in deeds involving him—it was a form of advertising. Until George Wall bought the seventy-five acres and the island from Isaiah Quinby in 1801, there was little happening here. With the growth of the economy in the early nineteenth century, the area became more attractive, and Nathaniel Saxton was one of the first to appreciate that.

THE SAXTONVILLE MILL

By 1814, while the War of 1812 was still going strong and the British blockade was being tightened, the coastal states, including New Jersey, were beginning to suffer from want of trade. Up until this time, the population was rapidly increasing, banks were being established and manufactures were thriving. This was when Nathaniel Saxton invested in Saxtonville. Then the war came, and by 1814, the economy had slowed down enough to hurt. This might have motivated Nathaniel Saxton and George Holcombe to find a way to make some money out of the old Cooper and Curry mill. Of the two partners, Holcombe was most in need.

On July 1, 1814, Nathaniel Saxton sold his half share in the ten-acre mill lot to George Holcombe, now living in New Brunswick, for $7,000. On the next day, Holcombe sold the entire mill lot to Myndert Wilson Jr. of Amwell for $13,000. This gave Holcombe a profit of $6,000, but it was only a paper profit, because Holcombe gave a mortgage to Wilson in the amount of $6,000 on the day after the deed was signed. He also conveyed his half interest in the thirty-acre lower half of Bull's Island to Nathaniel Saxton for $1,000. This was the last of Holcombe's property in Raven Rock. In December 1815, Nathaniel Saxton sold the whole island to William and Joseph Dilworth of Bucks County for $4,800.

Myndert Wilson Jr. was born on July 16, 1783, to Myndert Wilson Sr. and Jane Van Arsdalen. He first appears in Hunterdon County in 1809 as a resident of "Reading" (Readington) when he and wife Ann sold land there to Nicholas Ott. In this and future deeds, his name was usually spelled "Mindert." He was an unusually itinerant land investor, living in Bridgewater in 1814, when he sold a lot there, and being a resident of Amwell four months later, when he purchased the Raven Rock mill lot.

In March 1815, after less than a year, Wilson exchanged the mill lot for a farm in Kingwood and moved to Flemington, where he briefly owned a tavern. The next year, 1816, he was in New Brunswick, but by 1818, he was back in Readington. Next, he moved to a farm in Hopewell, but shortly afterward, he was in Montgomery Township, Somerset County, where his wife, Ann Wilson, died. Wilson then sold a farm in Amwell to his father and never again appeared in the Hunterdon County land records. James Major of Kingwood, the new owner of the mill, married Elizabeth Kerr on April 4, 1792, at the Presbyterian church in Abington, Bucks County, Pennsylvania. In 1803, they moved to a farm in Kingwood Township, adjoining the old farm of Isaiah Quinby. Major was close to the Quinby family, not just as a neighbor but also as a friend. In 1807, he witnessed the will of Isaiah Quinby, and in 1811, he witnessed the will of Quinby's widow, Miriam. Major's own daughter, born in about 1805, was also named Miriam.

In March 1815, James Major and his second wife, Frances, exchanged properties with Mindert Wilson. Wilson paid Major $3,471 for his Kingwood Township farm, and Major paid Wilson $13,000 for the mill at Saxtonville. Wilson gave Major a mortgage on the mill lot and another lot of ten acres, and George Holcombe gave Major another mortgage. The two notes were then cancelled, and a new mortgage for $6,000 was given to Major by Mindert Wilson. Less than two years later, James Major sold the mill lot to John R. Hamilton of Princeton for the same price he paid Wilson, but there was no mortgage recorded for Hamilton.

John R. Hamilton did take possession of the mill, for in 1818 a petition was made for a road from Prallsville to Saxtonville, which began at the millrace for the gristmill owned by John R. Hamilton. But soon after that, Hamilton disappeared. He didn't bother to sell the mill and probably became an "absconding debtor," like so many others during the Panic of 1819. In October 1819, the State Bank at New Brunswick sued James Major to recover principal and interest on the mortgage given by Mindert Wilson Jr. to George Holcomb in 1814. In April 1820, when the mill lot was sold at public auction, the deed made no mention of John R. Hamilton.

Meanwhile, George Holcombe had gone into bankruptcy. His original mistake was giving the millers Cooper and Curry a mortgage of $6,000, which was never paid, but he was also overextended on his many other properties. To solve this problem, he borrowed even more. In 1814, he got a mortgage from the State Bank at New Brunswick on his property at Headquarters for an astonishing $30,000. Then Holcombe turned around and gave Mindert Wilson the $6,000 mortgage for purchase of the Saxtonville mill lot.

By 1815, Holcombe could no longer maintain his balancing act. He left New Brunswick, moved back to Headquarters and assigned all his real estate and personal property to his brother, Samuel Holcombe Jr., of New Brunswick; his attorney, Nathaniel Saxton; and some friends. The bank sued Holcombe for his unpaid mortgage, and the court ordered the sale of the Headquarters property in 1817. By that time, Holcombe was sitting in debtors' prison in New York City, writing letters to Nathaniel Saxton in Flemington, looking for a way out of his predicament. Later, Holcombe retired to a farm in Kingwood until his remaining creditors got that property sold too. He ended his days, penniless and blind, at the home of his nephew, Theophilus Holcombe, in New Brunswick, dying on February 13, 1845.

After John R. Hamilton disappeared, the State Bank at New Brunswick sued for the outstanding mortgage, and the court ordered the sale of the mill lot at Saxtonville, "whereon Myndert Wilson formerly resided," along with a dwelling house, gristmill and sawmills. On March 17, 1820. John Bray bid on behalf of the bank and acquired the property for $4,000.

The bank was unable to find a buyer for the mill until April 1823, when Nicholas D. Baird, another "merchant of New Brunswick," purchased it for $5,525. The deed made no mention of either James Major or John R. Hamilton. On the same day, Baird and his wife, Susan, got a mortgage from the bank for the full amount of the purchase. Security for the mortgage was John Baird of Montgomery Township. Nicholas D. Baird was born in April 1797 in Griggstown, Somerset County, to John Baird and Catherine DuBois. He was only twenty-six when he bought the Saxtonville mill. He settled in the village with his wife and became part of the community.

In 1825, Baird was named one of the overseers of roads for Amwell Township. At a meeting of the county board of freeholders in May, Baird applied to view the road where it crosses the mouth of the "Niaaglan Creek" to see if a bridge was needed there. The freeholders agreed to meet at the house of William Johnson, who owned the tavern at Painter's Ferry. "Niaaglan Creek" was probably the Lockatong Creek (which has a long history of odd misspellings).

In July 1827, Baird announced in the *Gazette* that he and Oliver Creed, operating under the name of Baird and Creed at "Bool's Island," were dissolving their partnership "by mutual consent." Baird built a linseed oil mill at Saxtonville in the mid-1820s, perhaps in partnership with Oliver Creed, who was a resident of Trenton. Another of Baird's endeavors was to market patent rights for a cider maker, in partnership with cabinetmaker Isaac Lawshe.

During the presidential election of 1828, a contest between John Quincy Adams and Andrew Jackson, Baird began to dabble in politics. In April, he was as a candidate for the County Board of Freeholders but was not elected. In October, he joined the Committee of Vigilance of the National Republicans, the party supporting President Adams. Baird was named a delegate to the Republican State Convention in Trenton. Like Nathaniel Saxton, Baird wanted the federal government to spend more on canals, national roads and other improvements.

In April 1828, Baird bought the fifty-five-acre farm once owned by James Major, near Raven Rock, financed by a mortgage from David

Johnes of Headquarters, New Jersey. Shortly afterward, Baird bought the other farm of James Major, sixty-four acres in Kingwood on the Delaware River, including a share in the Green Briar Fishery.

Soon afterward, Baird failed to make payments on the mortgage for his mill lot. He was sued for debt in 1829 by James B. Cox. Despite this, Baird continued his political activity. He was one of many nominees for the New Jersey Assembly in September 1829. The following year, he was named a substitute delegate for the state convention to be held in Trenton. Meanwhile, things were moving slowly in the courts. A writ of fieri facias was issued by the chancery court in April 1830 to levy on the mill property, but Baird must have found a way to delay things as no action was taken immediately.

To raise money, Baird leased his sawmill to Richard Bennett in March 1831. The lease required that available water should go first to Baird's linseed oil mill before being run to the sawmill. Tragedy struck in April when Baird's wife, Susan, died in her early thirties. Her obituary in the *Hunterdon Gazette* read, "Died at Bool's Island, on the 16th instant, Mrs. Susan Baird, wife of Mr. N.D. Baird, aged 31 years." With the loss of his wife and his debts piling up, Baird became another in a long line of failures at the Saxtonville mill.

In 1831, the mill lot was seized by the State Bank at New Brunswick. At the sheriff's sale, James B. Cox was the highest bidder, offering $7,100. James Cox was acting in cooperation with the Delaware & Raritan Canal Company. Almost immediately after acquiring the mill lot, he sold it to Robert F. Stockton, the president of the company, for $10,192.

In August 1831, the National Republicans of Amwell Township chose Baird to be a delegate to the county convention to be held in September. He was then sued by his fellow delegate John Barber to recover the mortgage from David Johnes for the fifty-five-acre farm in Kingwood Township. James B. Cox sued him for the mortgage on the sixty-four-acre farm, which was sold at public auction in January 1832. Baird's fifty-five acres was sold in December 1833, at the house of Richard Bennett, innkeeper of Amwell.

During this time, life in Saxtonville was messy and uncomfortable. Construction of the feeder canal had begun early in 1832, starting at the northern end of Bull's Island and running the whole length of Bull's Creek. Even worse was an outbreak of cholera in the summer of 1832. Its victims were mostly canal workers. Those who died from the disease were buried in unmarked graves at various places along the canal. Ashbel Welch, who was in charge of construction, acted quickly to establish public health policies to contain the epidemic, which had ended by the following summer.

With so much misfortune, Nicholas D. Baird was probably glad to leave Hunterdon County. In 1850, he was living in a hotel in Mullica, Atlantic County, age forty-nine, working as a schoolteacher. By 1860, he was in Hillsborough, Somerset County, where he died on December 17, 1875, at the age of eighty-two.

Aerial photograph of Raven Rock and Lumberville in 1938. This is a rare view of the quarry and the millpond that ran from the base of Quarry Road toward the northwest of the village. The millpond was a source of water for the steam locomotives that stopped here and a nuisance to the neighbors due to mosquitoes. *Courtesy of Bill Tinsman.*

The Canal Company had no interest in running a mill. It advertised it for sale in December 1834 as "Bull's Island Mill Property…with Grist Mill, Saw Mill, four Dwelling Houses, a Stone Building formerly used as an Oil Mill, and a building formerly used as a Saw Mill, and also the Machinery belonging to the two latter buildings." With totally unwarranted optimism, the ad continued: "The above mills are at the head of the Delaware and Raritan Canal Feeder, and are well known to be among the best stands for business on the Delaware." Those interested were invited to contact Ashbel Welch, engineer, in Lambertville. No sale ever took place, and milling operations ceased. The property remained in the possession of Robert F. Stockton until long after his death in 1866.

SAXTONVILLE TAVERN'S FIRST INNKEEPER

The old stone building known as the Saxtonville Tavern was the home of Moses Quinby as early as 1785. He kept a store there during his tenure, which ended in 1815. After Nathaniel Saxton took possession, most people assume that he opened a tavern, but there is no evidence for this. There are applications for licenses for the Centre Bridge (Stockton) Tavern, for Johnson's Tavern at Painter's Ferry and the Rittenhouse Tavern in Rosemont, but none for Saxtonville. There was no need for a tavern at Raven Rock until construction began on the canal feeder.

The earliest mention of the building being used as a tavern comes in 1833, when a sheriff's sale was advertised to occur at the house of Richard Bennett, innkeeper of Amwell. This is also the earliest reference to Richard Bennett as an innkeeper. Richard Bennett (or "Bennet") had leased the sawmill at Saxtonville from Nicholas Baird in 1831. Just as Baird was losing control of the mill, construction began on the D&R Canal feeder. This was a great opportunity for a local innkeeper, since both travelers and canal workers were frequently found in taverns. Bennett probably applied to Saxton for a lease on the old stone house for just this purpose.

In 1834, Thomas Gordon compiled his *Gazetteer of the State of New Jersey*. Bull's Island merited a brief entry: "Bull's Island in the Delaware River, 23 miles above Trenton, near Saxtonville. The feeder of the Delaware and Raritan canal communicates with the Delaware here." There was no mention of Saxtonville.

By 1836, with the canal completed and in full operation, Nathaniel Saxton sold "All that certain Tavern House and lot of 11 acres" to his tenant, Richard Bennett of Amwell, for $1,100, including frontage of 495 feet on Bull's Creek. Richard Bennett was the son of Isaac Bennett, of Greenwich Township, Sussex County, who moved to Alexandria Township in 1837. A deed of 1842 lists his heirs, including Richard Bennett of Amwell.

Saxton was either extremely shrewd or extremely lucky. At the time of the sale, properties were valuable in Saxtonville, with the canal bringing lots of business. But soon afterward, everything came crashing down in the Panic of 1837. Had Saxton waited until then, he wouldn't have found a buyer. It would be several years before the economy rebounded.

On June 15, 1836, the commissioners of the Lumberville Bridge Company (once a dream of Nathaniel Saxton's, now a reality) advertised the sale of stock in the company. The books would be open "at the house of Richard Bennett." In 1838, a public sale of real estate was advertised to be held "at the inn of Richard Bennett in the township of Amwell." Later that year, another sale was advertised at the "inn of Richard Bennet"—only this time, the location was Delaware Township, for in the interval, Amwell Township had been divided by the state legislature into three new townships, Delaware being one of them. In January 1839, another sale was advertised "at the house of Richard Bennet Innkeeper at Bool's Island." None of these announcements used the name of Saxtonville. Now that Nathaniel Saxton was no longer the primary landholder, the name was fading away.

Richard Bennett expanded the old Quinby house with additional rooms and a grand two-story porch. But by 1839, Bennett was "desirous to go to the West." In November, he advertised the tavern and storehouse at the head of the canal feeder, "where he now lives," for sale. "The improvements are a large and commodious Tavern House, Store House, an excellent Shed and Barn all newly built," on eleven acres. He foresaw the arrival of the train from Belvidere to Trenton and claimed that "Bool's Creek is now becoming one of the best harbors for rafts on the river, which will afford a good opportunity for the lumbering business."

No satisfactory buyer responded, so Bennett gave up his plans to "go to the West." He finally found a buyer for his tavern lot ten years later. In 1848, Bernard Rogan of Tinnicum, Bucks County, bought the tavern

Saxtonville Tavern, as it has long been known. Although owned by Nathaniel Saxton from 1810 to 1836, it did not operate as a tavern until 1833. Its first owner, Richard Bennett, installed the handsome porch that is now gone. *Courtesy of Historic American Buildings Survey, after 1933.*

house and lot for $2,000. The Bennetts moved to Solebury Township in Bucks County, where Richard was a merchant in 1850 and a storekeeper living near Lumberville in 1860.

LATER INNKEEPERS

Bernard Rogan and his wife, Mary, were born in Ireland in about 1809. By 1834, they were living in Pennsylvania, where their children were born. Apparently, the Rogan name was pronounced quite differently from its spelling. When the *Cornell Map of 1851* was published, it showed the name as "B. Rorgaman's Hotel." Business was probably good at the tavern and "hotel," once the economy had recovered from the Panic of 1837. Things improved even more when construction began on the Belvidere & Delaware Railroad in 1851. The tracks were to run on the old towpath of the D&R Canal, which was still in business. A new towpath was needed, and it was constructed on the river side of the canal. Once again, Raven Rock was subjected to the turmoil and inconvenience of major construction, this time for three years, as the railroad did not open until 1854. But apparently, this turned out not so well for the tavern. One writer stated that the train passed the tavern and usurped the canal traffic, which had favored the tavern. This may be because the Raven Rock train station was located at the southern end of the village, whereas the tavern was closest to the northern end of the feeder canal.

After Bernard Rogan died in about 1855, wife Mary took over the hotel, no doubt with help from her children, who were now adults. A sale was advertised in December 1855 to be held "at the house of Mary Rogan in Delaware Twp." By 1860, Mary Rogan had found a tenant to run the tavern. Horace Smith, age thirty-six, was listed in the census as "Hotel Keeper," with wife Sallie (Sarah A. Paxson), age twenty-five, and daughter Isabella, age two. Meanwhile, the railroad was making significant changes to the way of life along the Delaware River. It ended the era of the Durham boat, which had been used to transport coal from the Lehigh Valley. The last trip by a Durham boat down the Delaware took place in 1865. One of Raven Rock's oldest residents, Joseph Rodman, was known for his skill in building Durham boats. Rodman died in 1849, and no one replaced him. Clearly, times were changing.

Mary Rogan probably died in 1866, for in December 1866, the heirs of Bernard Rogan sold the tavern house and eleven acres to Ruth S. Bray "of Saxtonville." This was Ruth Scott Bray, widow of John Bray (who died on February 24, 1866).

John Bray (1788–1866), of Kingwood Township, was the son of John Bray (1756–1845) and Rachel Rittenhouse (1760–1799). Ruth Scott was the daughter of James Scott (circa 1780–1850) and Mary Rittenhouse (born circa 1783). Mary was the niece of Rachel Rittenhouse. John Bray and Ruth Scott married in 1816 and had nine children. By 1850, only the youngest remained at home. Son Austen, age twenty, was helping his father on his farm, while younger brother Anderson Bray, eighteen, was a "cigar maker."

In the 1860 census, John and Ruth Bray were advanced in age, he seventy-one and she sixty-one years old, living with daughter Harriet, twenty-three, who would marry William H. Barcroft in 1863 and live for a while at the farm of her father-in-law, James Barcroft, at the corner of Route 519 and Strimples Mill Road. The ruins of the James Barcroft house are still standing.

Ruth Bray moved to Saxtonville after her husband's death, perhaps to join one of her sons who might have been running the tavern for Mary Rogan. And yet, by 1868, Ruth Bray was "of Kingwood" when the *Hunterdon County Democrat* published this item:

> *Intelligent Dog. Mrs. Ruth Bray of Kingwood, has a dog that is very handy around the house. He carries letters and packages between her home and that of her sons, at Bull's Island, a distance of three miles, with great punctuality and faithfulness, and manifests a disposition to be useful that commends itself as a model to a great many bipeds.*

Egbert T. Bush wrote that Austin Bray ran the tavern and was the last to do so. But by 1870, Austen Bray was a farmer living in Franklin Township, and his mother, Ruth, was a resident of Delaware Township, near Sergeantsville. Only one of her other sons was living in Delaware Township in 1870, but he was a farm laborer, not an

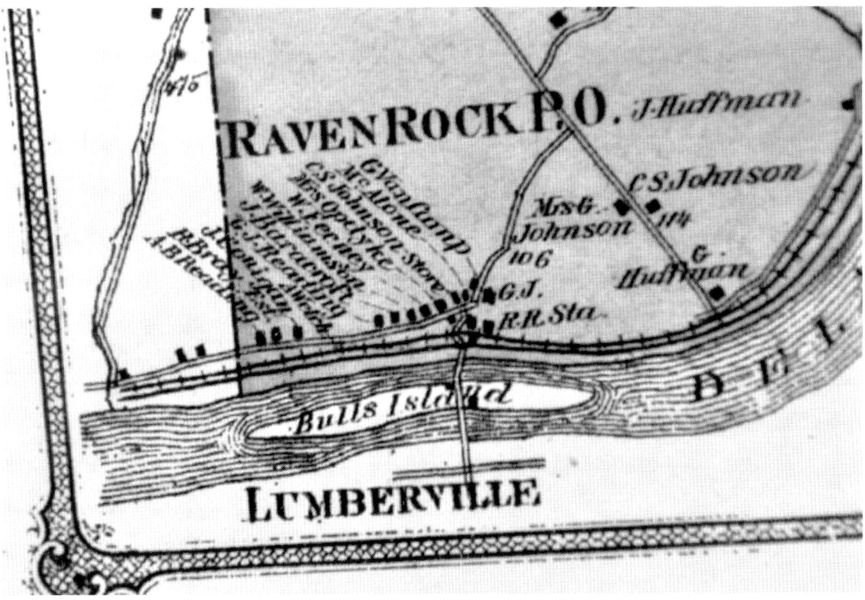

Map of Raven Rock, 1860. The map indicates the numerous stores and residents on both sides of the river due to economic growth brought about by the railroad and the new bridge. Lake, D. Jackson and Silas N. Beers, *1860 Map of the Vicinity of Philadelphia and Trenton. Courtesy of Goodspeedhistories.com.*

innkeeper. So it seems that inn keeping came to an end in Raven Rock about 1868.

Ruth Bray died on July 2, 1873, "at an advanced age, at her residence in Delaware Township." She was buried next to her husband at the Rosemont Cemetery. When the *Beers Atlas of Hunterdon County* was published that year, it showed the tavern lot as "R. Bray Estate." There was no "hotel" in Saxtonville.

Mrs. Bray's estate was insufficient to cover her obligations, so a sheriff's sale was ordered held. The *Democrat* reported that "the old tavern stand at Bull's Island sold to Thomas McAlone for $750," quite a bit less than the $2,000 that Bernard Rogan had paid. The fact that readers would understand the reference to "the old tavern stand" suggests that it hadn't been closed very long.

With the arrival of the canal and then the railroad, life in Saxtonville in the early nineteenth century was challenging but also exciting. The people who came to live there took risks to make a better life for themselves and their families. Some succeeded and others failed, but the village of Raven Rock (Saxtonville) remained a special place.

The Bridges of Raven Rock

Deborah Bodnar

The history of development in the Delaware River Valley largely revolved around river transportation. Before there were roads, canals or railroads, the only way to get the products to larger markets was via the river. In the very early days of the country, river activity increased with the spring thaw. Snow melt and seasonal rains increased the river depth to a point that rafts and Durham boats, the standard freight haulers of the river, could bring ore, farm produce, fur and timber from up the river to the downstream markets of Philadelphia.

However, the Delaware proved to be difficult to navigate and commercialize. It was too shallow in spots, the depth dropping even farther during the summer months. It was also too turbulent, containing a variety of rapids and rifts that posed the threat of capsizing. Ultimately, it was these difficulties that saved the Delaware from industrial degradation and allowed it to retain its natural beauty and join the list of federally designated "wild and scenic rivers."

Late Eighteenth Century

Before bridges existed, the only way to cross the Delaware was by ferry. Ferries originated at locations of commercial activity such as mills, fisheries or quarries, as well as on established traveling routes between major communities such as New York or Philadelphia via Flemington, New Brunswick or Trenton.

During the colonial era, ferry operations were franchises established by royal grant to individuals, often to reward loyalty to the Crown. One could not operate a ferry without such a grant. The object of the franchise was to make money by charging a toll to cross. Limiting the number of franchises was a means of preventing competition and ensuring profitability. In addition, ferries could and did have different owners on the two riverbanks, and ownership passed through multiple hands over time.

RAVEN ROCK FERRY—SOUTH (1775–1840)

A ferry crossing directly between Raven Rock and Lumberville, Pennsylvania, never existed. The ferry crossing was located roughly three quarters of a mile south of Bull's Island at what is now the intersection of Federal Twist Road and State Highway 29. It connected to Lumberton, Pennsylvania, at the mouth of the Cuttalossa Creek. On the New Jersey side, there was a local tavern that serviced travelers, and on the Pennsylvania side, there was a successful sawmill and quarry. The ownership and name of this ferry on both sides changed numerous times during its existence.

The New Jersey side of the ferry passed through the ownership in the following sequence: circa 1775–85 it was McClain's Ferry (Jacob McClain); circa 1785 it was Thorne's Ferry (Robert Thorn[e]); circa 1801–5 it was Painter's Ferry (Jacob Painter); circa 1805 it was Johnson's Ferry (Martin Johnson).

ADVENT OF BRIDGES

As the volume of interstate commerce and travel increased, the ferries proved to be inadequate for the job. Often they were not large enough to carry a coach and horse nor able to carry multiple carriages. By the end of the eighteenth century, busier crossings such as Trenton, Easton and Stockton had lines of travelers waiting to cross. A further disadvantage of ferries was their seasonal limitations. Ferries could not make the crossing in times of flood, low water or winter freeze. Eventually, crossing by ferry simply became dangerous. As the traffic of large, fast-moving and uncontrollable timber rafts increased, the risk of collision with the slower-moving ferries rose proportionately. Horses, too, were not naturals on the water, many spooking and jumping overboard with carriage attached, and some drowning before they could be freed.

Bridges were the solution to these various problems. Bridges held clear advantages over ferries, avoiding the limitations of weather and seasonal variations, as well as the dangers of commercial river traffic. The concept of tolled river crossings established with the ferries set a precedent that carried over to the eventual construction of bridges. Bridges could only be built by charters granted and approved by the joint legislatures of the states involved. They were to be privately owned corporations of local stockholders. The bridges were expected to charge a toll and make a profit. In addition, the corporation was responsible for bridge maintenance and repair. Should the bridge suffer damage or complete destruction in one of the river's inevitable floods, the corporation was to repair or rebuild the bridge. Since most bridges were moneymakers, the repairs or reconstruction were undertaken.

LUMBERVILLE–RAVEN ROCK BRIDGE (1835–1856)

The first bridge charters to be awarded in Hunterdon County went to the villages of Stockton and Lambertville in 1812. Both bridges, wooden covered structures, were operational in 1814. A competing petition for a bridge at Raven Rock–Bull's Island from Nathaniel Saxton, an early colonial land investor, proved unsuccessful. A charter for a bridge connecting Raven Rock–Bull's Island and Lumberville, Pennsylvania, was eventually approved by Pennsylvania and New Jersey in 1835 and 1836, respectively. The 1834 opening of the Delaware & Raritan Canal made such a bridge more advantageous for investors. Until this point, despite the existence of a tavern, fisheries, a sawmill and a gristmill, growth at Raven Rock–Bull's Island and Lumberville had been stymied.

The Lumberville-Delaware Bridge Company was formed shortly after the approval of the charter, but actual construction languished for

Skaters on the Delaware River enjoy a rare opportunity. The whole river is frozen solid. This view was created before the flood of 1903, when a section of the Lumberville–Raven Rock Bridge was washed downriver. *Courtesy of Bill Tinsman.*

almost twenty years. Whether there was difficulty in obtaining financing or conflicting viewpoints over the bridge's location and design, the cause for the delay remains obscure. The delay did have one distinct advantage, sparing the bridge from the destruction wrought by the major flood of 1841. The need for a bridge connecting Lumberville to the New Jersey shore in Raven Rock became more pressing in the early 1850s, when the Belvidere & Delaware Railroad passed through the hamlet and a station was erected in Raven Rock.

The bridge contract was awarded to Major Anthony Fry of Lumberville and Solon Chapin of Easton, Pennsylvania, in 1853. Solon Chapin was the head engineer. He was also responsible for the construction of bridges at Riegelsville, Pennsylvania, and Belvidere, New Jersey. Construction began in 1853, and the bridge opened for business in 1856. An 1857 supplement to the original charter exempted churchgoers from paying the toll on the Sabbath. The bridge remained tolled until 1932, when it was purchased by the Joint Commission for the Elimination of Toll Bridges Over the Delaware River. This agency, created by joint legislation in New Jersey and Pennsylvania in

The stone tollhouse built next to the first bridge over the Delaware River between Lumberville, Pennsylvania, and Raven Rock, New Jersey. The house is located in Lumberville, Pennsylvania. The bridge was opened in 1856 and was closed in 1944. *Collection of Deb Bodnar.*

1912–13, acquired bridges from private owners at a price agreeable to the stockholders and freed them of tolls. This joint commission operated and maintained the bridges with public funds provided by both states.

The bridge was typical of the wooden covered construction of the day—seven hundred feet in length and four spans long, one of which crossed over the Pennsylvania Canal. The final cost of the bridge was $22,000. It included a budgeted expense for several barrels of rum for the workmen. More than muscle and money was necessary to build a bridge! There was a stone residential structure on the Pennsylvania end of the bridge. It served as the home for the toll collectors and, later, for the bridge police of the joint bridge commission. While never as busy as neighboring bridges in Stockton or Lambertville, the bridge served the Lumberville and Raven Rock communities without problems until the Pumpkin Freshet of 1903.

1903 FLOOD: THE PUMPKIN FRESHET

A "freshet" was the term used by early settlers of the Delaware Valley to describe the increased depth in the river caused by snowmelt and seasonal rains. But settlers also used the term to refer to the major, killer floods that destroyed bridges, floated houses, ruined crops and ended lives. The October 1903 Pumpkin Freshet was one such flood. It started raining on Thursday, October 8, and when the skies cleared the following Monday, the flood level was ten feet higher than the record-setting 1841 flood. All bridges across the Delaware between Belvidere and Trenton were either washed away or severely damaged. The New Hope–Lambertville and Yardley bridges went out. The Point Pleasant–Byram Bridge, one of the largest iron bridges over the river, was struck by pieces of one of the upriver bridges and demolished.

The flood washed away one of the river spans of the Lumberville–Raven Rock Bridge on October 10, 1903. The Stockton Center Bridge survived the flood undamaged and served the Raven Rock and Lumberville communities during the interim. The damaged span was replaced by a steel truss in 1904, and the bridge was back in business. The bridge, two-thirds old timber and one-third steel, remained that way until 1947.

BULL'S ISLAND HOSTS WORLD WAR II BRIDGE EXERCISE (1942)

In July 1942, Raven Rock was "invaded" by the Seventieth Engineer Company from Camp DuPont in Delaware. Its members were accompanied by an infantry company. The purpose of the "invasion" was to train in the rapid erection of light pontoon bridges under simulated war conditions to prepare troops for actual warfare. Designed to bear up to ten tons in capacity, these bridges allowed a light tank, small artillery and trucks to make a crossing. Over several days of maneuvers, the troops were able to cut their bridge building time in half.

Raven Rock was chosen because the river offered ideal training conditions: a fourteen-foot channel and a swift six-miles-per-hour current. In addition, the campground on Bull's Island could accommodate the

Pontoon Bridge, July 1942. The U.S. Army conducted an exercise during which it built several pontoon bridges across the Delaware River near Raven Rock. During this time, the troops used Bull's Island for their encampment. Locals were entertained by the exercises; however, the army's use of the covered bridge was detrimental to the structure. *Courtesy of Luverne Updegrove Caulton.*

troops' pup tents. About 150 engineers and 70 support troops participated in the exercises, providing the local residents with a much-enjoyed break from life's daily routine.

CLOSING OF THE LUMBERVILLE–RAVEN ROCK BRIDGE (1944–1947)

During repair work to the nose of the first river pier in 1943, it was discovered that the entire superstructure, with the exception of the steel truss, was severely deteriorated and subject to collapse. A thorough inspection found the ninety-year-old bridge rotted beyond repair. It was deemed unsafe for vehicular traffic in February 1944 and was closed entirely in June 1945. This left the residents of Raven Rock without a direct route to the shops, churches and post office in Lumberville. The situation left the Lumberville residents without direct access to the railroad station in Raven Rock. The closest alternatives were Centre

Bridge in Stockton or the Point Pleasant–Byram Bridge, both about three miles in either direction.

A few enterprising young men of Raven Rock saw this situation as an opportunity to be good Samaritans. Kenneth and Robert Scarborough and Floyd Updegrove provided a free daily rowboat ferry service for the residents of the two communities. Other Raven Rock residents were not so sanguine. Some blamed the bridge's deterioration and lengthy closure on members of the local artist community whom they accused of opposing maintenance or replacement of the bridge because of its picturesque nature. It was more likely that the delay was due to the lack of building materials for peacetime purposes as a result of the country's World War II efforts. There was hope for a new bridge at the war's end, when steel once again became available. In the meantime, the Delaware River Joint Toll Bridge Commission (DRJTBC) decided that the traffic volume at the Lumberville–Raven Rock location didn't warrant a vehicular bridge. Plans to replace it with a bridge designed solely for pedestrian traffic went forward.

The DRJTBC, established in 1934 by joint legislation enacted by New Jersey and Pennsylvania, had succeeded the Joint Commission for the Elimination of Toll Bridges Over the Delaware River. At the time, the original joint commission was buying the privately owned toll bridges, no one envisioned the impact that mass-produced automobiles and trucks would have on the economic and social patterns of American life. The agency evolved due to the tremendous increase in interstate motor vehicle traffic post–World War I and due to the need for larger, stronger bridges capable of accommodating this new mobile society. Its mission became one of maintaining the aging state-owned "free bridges" and building, operating and maintaining a network of modern superhighway toll crossings.

THE ROEBLING PEDESTRIAN BRIDGE (1947)

In 1947, the famed John A. Roebling & Sons, Company, Trenton-based designer and builder of the Brooklyn Bridge, was looking for ways to capitalize on its reputation to expand its operations in the postwar economy. The company secured the state contract to replace the 1856

Lumberville–Raven Rock Pedestrian Bridge, built by John A. Roebling's Sons Company in 1947. *Photo by R. Curt Chinnici.*

Lumberville–Raven Rock covered bridge. Roebling got its first chance to build a public cable–stiffened bridge, an innovation Roebling engineers developed during World War II. Roebling engineers first removed the entire superstructure. The substructure, the original 1856 piers and abutments, were found to be in good condition and were not replaced. The company designed a five-span modern suspension bridge with stiffened cables carrying a prestressed, precast concrete walkway floor. Its total cost was $75,000.

THE GREAT FLOOD OF 1955

In August 1955, the East Coast was buffeted by two major hurricanes only days apart, bringing disaster to the Delaware River Valley. Hurricane Connie, which hit the North Carolina coast on August 12, wasn't initially forecast to reach the Northeast. Hurricane warnings for the region were cancelled. But Connie, a trickster, turned north, crashed into the mid-Atlantic, moved east to west through New Jersey and Pennsylvania and deflated over Lake Erie. It dumped ten inches of rain in the Delaware Valley over two days, saturating the ground and leaving the rivers near flood stage. July 1955, however, had been extremely dry, so the water was welcomed.

Hurricane Diane followed up the coast on August 17. Although losing the force of its winds as it proceeded north, it did not lose its rain. Between August 18 and 19, the Hunterdon County area received an additional four to five inches of rain on watersheds unable to absorb it. When it was over, the river had crested at 30.4 feet in Stockton, 191 people were dead, 600 Hunterdon County residents were homeless and damages were estimated at $1.6 billion. Records had been broken. The high-water mark surpassed that of the 1903 Pumpkin Freshet.

The floodwaters, with its floating debris, damaged every bridge up and down the Delaware River to varying degrees. These conditions presented unanticipated challenges to the DRJTBC. During several hours of the crisis, the only DRJTBC Bridge open to traffic was the Trenton-Morrisville (Route 1) toll bridge. Four "free" bridges were completely destroyed, among them the Point Pleasant–Byram steel truss bridge. It was not replaced. Of the remaining three bridges, the Easton-Phillipsburg Bridge was the only one fully restored. The Yardley-

Floodwaters on Saint Patrick's Day 1936, with (from left) the Williamson House, the Johnson-Feeney House and the Opdyke House. The photo is taken from the railroad station. *Courtesy of Luverne Updegrove Caulton.*

Wilburtha Bridge opened briefly until it was declared unsafe for further use in 1961. The Portland-Columbia Bridge, the grand dame of covered bridges, was replaced with a steel girder design in 1958.

THE FLOODS OF 2004, 2005 AND 2006

Weather patterns in the Delaware River Valley were fairly benign for more than fifty years, with no major flooding until a series of storms in 2004, 2005 and 2006 once again sent the waters raging down the Delaware. The remnants of Hurricane Ivan interacted with a weather front between September 17 and September 18, 2004, dumping heavy rain across northwest New Jersey and New York's Catskill Mountains. A particularly moist July had created the conditions for flooding: ground near saturation point, higher than average stream flows and reservoirs near capacity. The water crested at 22.5 feet in Stockton, its highest level since the Great Flood of 1955. While the flood did not affect the Lumberville–Raven Rock Bridge, it did serious damage to Bull's Island State Park. The pavement on both sides of the canal bridge at the entrance to the park was undermined. The campgrounds were littered with downed trees, debris and sand deposits, necessitating its closure. It was hoped to have them ready for the spring 2005 camping season, which was when the weather struck again, less than a year after Hurricane Ivan's blow.

The flood of April 2005, while not surpassing the Great Flood of 1955, was its closest rival. The three conditions necessary to produce a flood were present: heavy rainfall over a short period to time, saturated ground due to earlier rain and snow melt and reservoirs at capacity. The crest at Stockton was measured at 26.7 feet. However, unlike Ivan, the floodwaters crossed Route 29, put several inches of water in Raven Rock homes and forced residents to evacuate.

The final hammer blow came in June 2006. It was a repeat scenario, only this time the crest was slightly less than 2005. Stockton measured a high-water mark of 25.4 feet. The devastation remained the same: lives disrupted, homes inundated, damage and destruction in the hundreds of millions of dollars and a lengthy cleanup.

Pressures of development and the expected increase in hurricane activity over the foreseeable future create an ongoing challenge for public policy planners. It will be up local elected officials working in conjunction with appropriate state and federal agencies to create a watershed management plan that will mitigate the threat of major flooding in the wild and scenic Delaware River Valley.

THE BRIDGE SURVIVES

Through it all, the Roebling-designed Lumberville–Raven Rock Bridge has survived. The bridge successfully weathered the Great Flood of 1955 with minor damage when others were washed away. But the stresses of nature and repeated battering by floodwaters filled with debris exacted a cost. In 1993, the entire bridge deck was reconstructed, a new lighting system was installed, approach ways were made handicapped accessible and the abutments, wingwalls and all river piers were repointed.

At the 2010 annual bridge inspection, engineers found the bridge safe for public use but in overall poor condition. The Delaware River Joint Toll Bridge Commission (DRJTBC) has a planned rehabilitation project scheduled for late winter/spring 2013, a date chosen to accommodate the Lumberville business community. The rehabilitation is intended to improve conditions such that sustained public closures won't be necessary for fifteen years into the future.

The bridge today, once an essential link for civic and commercial interaction between two communities, is used primarily for recreational purposes. It still connects the villages of Raven Rock and Lumberville, but now the area is a tourist destination. Bull's Island, as well as the canals on both sides of the river, has become part of the respective state park systems. Hikers, bicyclists and kayakers enjoy the area year round, and everyone takes a moment to relish the view from the middle of the Roebling jewel over the Delaware.

Navigating the River at Raven Rock

Jeffrey L. Adams

In the tongue of the Leni-Lenape People, the great Delaware River was known as Lenapewihittuk. Translated to English, it means literally, "Our River." The Lenapes referred to themselves as common people and enjoyed a peaceable way of life near the river.

While inhabiting the areas of Bull's Island and Raven Rock, the Lenapes did not ply the river with canoes and birch skiffs with bows of hickory, the way that popular culture would eventually portray them. Their New England and New York relatives, however, did utilize these methods.

On the occasion that a canoe was in order, these west-central New Jersey natives burned out the hollow of a log. This conveyance, often called a dugout, was crude, awkward for navigating the Delaware and impossible for portage. Swift of foot, the Lenapes preferred their elders' footpaths for traveling distance.

Upon arriving in the Delaware Valley, Europeans discovered that the Lenapes had established an elaborate system of trails measuring eighteen inches in width. These paths through the wilderness accommodated those walking single file. Alternative paths were individually designated for warriors, messengers, hunters, diplomats or visiting families. These native passages through the thickets became bridle paths during the early years of the colonial period. Some stretched for hundreds of miles. As our young nation developed, native trails became the foundation for post roads and, eventually, our nation's highways.

At first, the early European settlers were pleased to have the Delaware River in such a strategic location. Flowing through four states, it formed a boundary between Pennsylvania and New Jersey and connected the inland portion of the colony of New York with the Delaware Bay.

However, this proposed avenue of commerce was practically useless for navigation because of its many rapids. One also had to consider the fluctuation in depth with spring freshets and summer dry spells. In the 1750s, folks were drawn to the edge of the river one morning by the sounds of a commotion. On the banks, people had doffed their hats and were shouting and waving. In some settlements, a church bell was heard. On the river, a group of Durham boats was drifting swiftly but silently downriver. This moment would signify a change in the lives of all citizens of the Delaware Valley. The great river had been conquered and could now be used for commerce.

Durham boats were designed at Riegelsville on the Pennsylvania side of the river. Robert Durham, an engineer at the Durham Iron Works, is given credit for this large river craft. Some historians feel that he borrowed the design from the Swedes, who were on the Delaware in the 1600s. Durham's boats could measure up to sixty-five feet in length and eight feet in width. Pointed at both ends, they resembled wooden canoes. Four oars propelled the boat, and a long sweep oar was mounted on the rear of the boat for navigation.

A thirty-foot mast mounted with a triangular sail completed this graceful vessel. On board, the load going downriver might be as heavy as seventeen tons. A typical load would be 150 barrels of flour or 600 bushels of corn. Many carried pig iron for foundries in Philadelphia. All types of raw material could now be marketed outside of the region.

Virtually anything that could be moved on the river was shipped on a Durham boat. The streets of Philadelphia and Wilmington were cobbled with stones brought downriver on Durham boats. On a return trip, upriver, the boat could haul a much smaller load and thus needed the assistance of iron-tipped poles to navigate the rapids. The boat contained a covered sleeping area and a small charcoal stove for warmth. Whiskey and applejack were stored aboard in the event of a medical emergency.

On Bull's Island, Nathaniel Saxton sold a plot of ground to Joseph Rodman near a distillery. Durham boats were brought aground for repair at this location. Records indicate that his repair operation grew to the

Durham boat navigating down a river with full sails on an inland river. Cargo is whiskey or molasses. These were also used to haul coal from the Lehigh region to markets along the Delaware River, such as Philadelphia or Trenton. Engraving, 1810. *Courtesy of University of Kentucky.*

point that Joseph Rodman actually began to build these boats on Bull's Island, and these were said to be of good quality.

The success of the Durham boat spread across the colonies and would become the standard vessel for river navigation for more than one hundred years. They were used in lakes, rivers and canals and were responsible for increasing water traffic in all regions of our growing nation. Yet the most enduring legacy of this workhorse was demonstrated in George Washington's choice of this craft when he forded the Delaware in a snowstorm to surprise the enemy at Trenton on December 26, 1776.

At about the same time that the Durham boat made its appearance, another craft began plying the Delaware River. In 1764, the first log raft was floated downstream from the upper reaches of the river. Daniel Skinner of Sullivan County, New York, conceived the idea of lashing trees together to form a raft. Bound for Philadelphia, the raft made it in just over a week, and the logs resulted in a tidy profit for the driver. On his next trip, he made it in two days. The city was growing, and the need for board lumber was insatiable.

The need for felled timber in all aspects of industry resulted in the river filling with rafts each spring as the river reached the depth necessary to propel rafts downstream. Boards were needed for the buildings and walkways, and early bridges were constructed with lumber; before the use of coal, wood was needed for heating. Additionally, the tannin obtained from the bark of trees was a necessary ingredient in the processing of leather.

Over the years, the size of rafts increased, as did the number of those seen passing on the river. The height of the rafting era was reached in the decade of 1875 to 1885. On occasion, 15 to 20 rafts could be viewed from Bull's Island on the river at one time. One record keeper counted 3,140 rafts between March and May 1885 at the Lackawaxen Dam.

The rafting era changed the whole face of the Delaware River. Ferries at one time had been commonplace for river crossings. Timber rafts put an end to the ferries because of the danger of collision. This hastened the building of bridges. Bridges also had to be constructed to accommodate the passage of rafts. The height of a bridge and the distance between piers had to be factored into the construction.

Log rafts lined up along the Pennsylvania shore of the Delaware River across from Bull's Island. The logs are to be brought up to the sawmill at Tinsman's Lumberyard and processed into building material. *Courtesy of Bill Tinsman.*

As the nineteenth century reached its end, rafts were becoming a rare sight on the Delaware River. Sawmills were built closer to the source of the lumber, and the rail industry had taken over much of the shipment of wood products. In the Upper Delaware region, the forests were clear-cut, and lumber in this area was all but gone.

A final outcry from the public came with the Great Flood of October 10, 1903. Rafts that had gone out of control destroyed several bridges on the Delaware. In 1913, the Mitchell boys of Callicoon claimed the distinction of taking the last raft ever floated down the Delaware River to market. It was run from Dillontown to Bordentown.

A few towns along the Delaware River gained great economic growth during the logging era. But the canals and the railroads would bring the greatest changes to life on the river. For the residents of Raven Rock, the most enduring reminder of lumbering on the river is at the other end of the footbridge from Bull's Island, in Lumberville, Pennsylvania. The beginnings of Tinsman's Lumber Yard can be traced to the first years that logs were first floated downriver. In 1869, William Tinsman purchased a lumber business that was more than one hundred years old at that time, and his family continues to operate it to this day.

The idea of connecting inland settlements by manmade waterways was not a new idea to the general public in the 1820s. George Washington had favored inland navigation and anticipated that this country would embrace this notion in the 1790s. It was not until after the completion of the Erie Canal across the state of New York in 1825 that the nation realized the impact of a canal on a state's economy.

When the Erie Canal was completed, the cost of transporting goods and passengers dropped an astounding 95 percent. The canal opened the Great Lakes to the eastern seaboard, which soon established the city of New York as a great financial center. The State of New York appeared to have a monopoly on the whole interior region of the country. Other state legislatures took note, and the nation was caught up in what seemed to be "canal frenzy."

At the same time, the State of New Jersey had already been presented with differing ideas of where to place an interstate waterway. The British had blockaded the Atlantic coast during the War of 1812, and it was the belief of many that an internal waterway would alleviate such difficulties if another war were to take place. This would also provide a safer and shorter route between the cities of New York and Philadelphia.

In 1816, a commission was appointed by the New Jersey legislature to determine a feasible route. This group included Canvass White, the builder of the Erie Canal. It was this commission's recommendation that a route should be excavated between the Delaware and Raritan Rivers. The legislature granted a charter based on its report.

In 1820, stock was authorized bearing the name of the Delaware & Raritan Canal Company. The stock sales fell just short of the $1 million needed to proceed, and the idea of a canal was shelved. There was a public outcry in New Jersey in 1825 when the newspapers of New Jersey and Philadelphia pointed out that the newly opened Erie Canal would cause an increase in conducting business to all other states because of toll roads.

The New Jersey legislature was once again pressured to consider the building of the New Jersey canal. In 1827, a "Convention for the Improvement of Internal New Jersey" was held at Princeton. This body of citizens implored the legislature to move forward with the proposed Delaware & Raritan Canal.

Canvass White once again was called on to draw up plans for a canal. The design called for it to be sixty-six miles long and seventy feet wide, connecting the Delaware and Raritan Rivers between New Brunswick and Bordentown. The depth of the canal would be eight feet. The plans included the least number of locks possible to provide quick passage of boats.

After fourteen years of delays, proposals and discussions, the New Jersey legislature passed an act on February 4, 1830, to charter the canal. Coupled with this ruling was a charter for the Camden & Amboy Railroad, which was one of the first lines laid in the country. Although the canal was authorized, the promoters of this operation found it impossible to raise the necessary funding. About $1 million was needed, and the public was skeptical of investing in the stock.

Two important Princeton investors stepped forward and brought $500,000 to the table. Commodore Robert F. Stockton and his father-in-law were strong believers in the viability of the canal. This capital was enough to allow the construction to begin. When completed, the final cost of the whole venture was almost $3 million, nearly triple the plans from the original 1816 survey. However, over the many years of operation, the canal would prove to be a great investment.

Excavation of the canal commenced in the summer of 1830 at Kingston, New Jersey. The building of the entire feeder canal fell under the jurisdiction of Ashbel Welch. Local laborers showed up to work on the canal along with a large number of recent immigrants, primarily from Ireland. Using picks and shovels, they began clearing a path. Every task was done by hand since there were no mechanical methods available. Mules were used to pull scrapers, which were crude earth-moving tools. The excavated soil and stone was piled on the bank to be fashioned into a towpath.

When the ditch reached its desired depth, the laborers cut slabs of clay to line the bottom of the canal. A slurry of sand, water and clay was pressed between the joints. The final step of walking on the seams and prodding the seams together with tools completed the job. All of this was done to prevent the water from leaving the canal by seeping into the ground.

Skilled craftsmen constructed the stone and ironwork on the spot. A blacksmith and his assistants were on hand to do finish work on bridges. They were also kept busy by repairing tools. Stonecutters were available, too. More than one hundred bridges and locks were built for the entire project. On Bull's Island, a recently dismantled distillery provided nicely finished stones for a bridge foundation. After four long years of intensive labor, the canal was opened with much fanfare. Aside from the actual money spent to complete the project, a great deal of human suffering through accidents and disease had taken its toll as well.

Sailors arriving from the West Indies brought back a strain of cholera in 1832 that spread throughout the countryside, as well as Raven Rock. The ones most susceptible to this disease were the canal workers living in squalid shanties along the feeder canal. Supervisor Ashbel Welch appointed a board of health to police townspeople to comply with sanitary measures, and the town of Princeton established an isolation hospital that helped to eradicate the problem of disease. The following winter, there were few cases reported. It is unfortunate that hundreds of laborers, mostly of Irish decent, never lived to see the celebration of their efforts. Locally, some were buried at a cemetery at Prallsville, and as late as the 1960s, one could visit a small graveyard on Bull's Island, which had as many as fifty crude markers honoring the lives of some who had fallen. Others, is has been said, were laid to rest along the path of the canal.

Canal workers posed at the head of the feeder canal. The Saxton-Heath House appears in the distance, on the right. In the upper left of the image is the split in the rock palisade of Raven Rock. *Courtesy of Bull's Island Ranger Station.*

The Delaware & Raritan Canal, in actuality, was a system composed of two separate waterways. The forty-mile main canal, which runs from New Brunswick to Brodentown, is fed by the twenty-two-mile feeder canal that begins at Bull's Island. The canal's source is the Delaware River, and the canal continues to Trenton in a relatively straight line. Although the design of the D&R Canal is one of a very level body of water, the main portion after the feeder canal is horseshoe shaped. The feeder canal provides a gravity flow and produces a momentum to push water through the entire system.

Originally, the feeder canal was intended as just a mechanical component of the canal operation; however, as the demand for anthracite coal increased, the D&R's sister canal on the Pennsylvania side of the river began hauling barges laden with coal from the Lehigh coalfields.

The Delaware division of the Pennsylvania Canal was completed in 1832 and paralleled the river through Bucks County. An intake lock was added to the D&R Canal at Lambertville, New Jersey. This allowed boats from the Pennsylvania side to be cable-ferried across the Delaware River. This route was a primary source for New York City and Philadelphia markets. With the Pennsylvania Canal being so dependent on its transfer to the D&R, it is ironic that when the feeder canal was first approved in 1830, Pennsylvania refused to grant permission to have water diverted from the Delaware River into the canal. There was a fear that this might reduce the depth of water in the lower river.

Boats also entered the feeder canal from the Delaware River at its source on the upper end of Bull's Island. The canal was fed water from a wing-dam that was built across the width of the river. Water was diverted into the mouth of the canal and flowed from this point through the system. Above the wing-dam, at Byram, New Jersey, the calm waters of the Delaware resemble a lake.

The canal continued to operate and adapt to changes over the years. Mules and barges gave way to steam and gasoline propulsion after the First World War. Rail traffic also took away a great deal of freight traffic that once used the canal. Pleasure boats appeared in the 1920s, and the public started to view the old canal as a place for leisure. In 1932, with little notice to the public, the canal ceased to operate. After three years of inactivity, ownership reverted to the state, as agreed in its charter. Today, it is used as a source for fresh water for communities in Mercer County, New Jersey.

During its years of operation, the Delaware & Raritan Canal provided its investors with unexpected profits. For nearly a century after, the D&R was considered one of the nation's busiest navigation canals. Business peaked during the 1860s and 1870s, when coal from Pennsylvania was hauled through New Jersey to facilitate New York's industrial growth.

Those who balked at supporting the canal never saw that this small operation would one day eclipse the great Pennsylvania Canal System in revenue. The D&R canal eventually hauled more freight than the Erie Canal. Today, it is one of the nation's greatest inland water trails and the most intact canal to survive from the great canal building era of the 1830s. The primary reason for its continued use lies in its maintenance by the Elizabethtown Water Company and the New Jersey Water Supply Authority, which keeps the water safe for drinking purposes.

Stories from Bull's Island Railroad Station

Jeffrey L. Adams

After World War II, popular culture began to grow nostalgic over the portrayal of the common rail depot and small rural train routes that serviced flag stop towns. Movies and television had recurring situations that focused on the community and its interaction with life at the train station. On the Belvidere & Delaware Railroad, Raven Rock had more than its fair share of colorful stories.

Located 22.8 rail miles north of Clinton Street in Trenton and 27.9 miles south of Phillipsburg, Raven Rock is close to the halfway point of these two terminal towns. However, the line continues on north to Belvidere, New Jersey, making connections to the Lehigh Valley, Pennsylvania coal fields. It is also a direct passenger and freight link to the northern tier of Pennsylvania and upstate New York. Consequently, much of the rolling stock at Raven Rock Station originated with the Lehigh Valley Rail Road. Daily, great lines of coal cars streamed by on the way south to connect to the industries of Philadelphia and New York.

The station at Raven Rock serviced passengers boarding from the two communities of Raven Rock and Lumberville, in Bucks County, Pennsylvania. Professional artists and people who had connections with theater or business in Manhattan lived within walking distance of the Lumberville–Raven Rock Bridge. They moved here because they were attracted to the seclusion of Bucks County and to the spectacular palisades on the Pennsylvania side of the Delaware.

The entrance to Bull's Island from Raven Rock Station was completely destroyed by the Pumpkin Freshet of 1903. Repair work began on the canal lock and to replace the bridge. Just behind the station is a large building that may have been a hotel. The crane in the photo is similar to those used to move stones in the quarry just behind the station on Quarry Road. *Collection of Jeffrey Adams.*

The Belvidere & Delaware Railroad was chartered on March 2, 1836; however, no stock was sold until 1848. Construction began in early spring of 1850, and tracks had reached Bull's Island Station by summer 1851. The official name of this stop would remain Bull's Island until October 24, 1890, when the designation was changed to Raven Rock.

Ashbel Welch was placed in charge of the construction of the railroad. Since he had surveyed and built the feeder source for the D&R canal, he knew that the optimum place to locate the rails would be on the berm of the feeder canal. This resulted in an amazingly level grade for the rail line, ensuring that trains could travel safely at fairly high speeds. Welch went on to become superintendent of this new railroad and served in this capacity for more than three decades.

An early steam locomotive, pulling wooden coaches, pauses at Bull's Island station. Two tracks allowed a train to continue on while the other train was boarding passengers or mail. A spur line left the mainline to enter the nearby quarry. For many years, the local post office was located within the railroad station. *Courtesy of Bill Tinsman.*

Reviewing a recorded timeline of activity on the Belvidere & Delaware Railroad gives an idea of the goings-on at Raven Rock over the years. Having the railroad as integral part of the community guaranteed that many unusual and exciting events would take place.

On August 27, 1870, a broadside was placed at the depot announcing that "Stove Pipe [hats] are making their appearance."

On April 1, 1872, the Pennsylvania Railroad (PRR) took over the operation of the Bel-Del. This great corporation was expanding all over the eastern half of the country and brought with it an operation that would soon be recognized as the as "the standard railroad of the world." By the following year, the PRR had sixteen additional locomotives added to the fleet, bringing the total number to forty-seven.

In May 1879, a small steamboat passed up the Delaware River. The boat was taken up the feeder canal and entered the Delaware at Bull's Island. The boat, christened the *Kittatinny*, could hold seventy-five passengers and plied the river at Port Jervis from the Delaware Gap.

Later, it was reported on June 27, 1879, that *Kittatinny* appeared to be an ill-fated craft. In attempting to ascend the Delaware at Port Jervis, it struck a rock near Milford, Pennsylvania, and was badly damaged. It was towed ashore, repaired and then returned to the Water Gap. The next Friday, a party of prominent gentlemen boarded it for a little excursion. The *Kittatinny* steamed out into the river, struck a rock and sank.

In the 1880s, President Grover Cleveland passed through Raven Rock on his way to Buffalo, New York, on a few occasions. On one occasion, the president detrained at Raven Rock and took a carriage across the river to the Black Bass, where he enjoyed fishing and a night's stay at the inn.

In the 1880s and 1890s, there were more than 4 million peach trees in New Jersey, with half of these located in Hunterdon County. At harvest time, the station swelled with those boarding the "Peach Express" headed for nearby orchards. Additional coaches were added to trains, and townspeople arrived with baskets in tow. People could earn extra money by filling pecks for the growers. Fruit was brought home for preserves and desserts. A blight that began in 1886 from California plums had killed most of the peach trees by 1920.

In 1890, it was noted that circus trains were always welcome on the tracks, but never on Sunday.

In May 1910, the Edison Film Corporation, filmed a classic short, "A Western Romance," at Raven Rock. The station conductor, Hoffman, and the depot are quite visible in this film. This Wild West adventure featured a number of cowboys and Indians.

The descendants of Raven Rock's founder, Isaiah Quinby, gathered at Bull's Island in June 1891 for their first annual reunion picnic. It was a novel scene—a family reunion and a picnic were held on board a train of cars on a siding at the station. A storm raged outside, but the extended family found the cars equipped with banquet tables and comfortable seating for an enjoyable day.

A post-1903 flood photograph shows a large building that resembles many railroad hotels of that era. It is situated within a few yards of the track and the Raven Rock Station. It is possible that this structure may have been used for guests or may have had some official function for the railroad company. The fact that the name "Ashbel Welch" appears among names of property owners on a map of Raven Rock during that period suggests that he had interest in the community. It was not unusual for railroad superintendents to invest in ventures along the rails that they controlled.

The Pennsylvania Railroad installed concrete telephone booths along the Bel-Del line. The railroad used a new type of telephone technology that utilized the steel rails to transmit telephone communications. They did not use regular telephone lines. Several of these concrete booths still exist as strange remnants of the Bel-Del line. *Photo by R. Curt Chinnici.*

At Raven Rock, for many years, children trekked up Quarry Road to a small country school in the township. When the eighth grade was completed, the Belvidere & Delaware Railroad provided passage to the Lambertville High School, where most locals completed their education.

The Pennsylvania Railroad introduced a new form of technology on Bel-Del lines after World War II. The most extensive train communication system in use utilized the tracks as an electronic network and carried signal to telephones throughout the locomotives. Managers of other branches rode the Bel-Del to see the equipment and quickly ordered it for their lines. In 1966, the system was replaced with radiophones.

After heavy usage during both world wars, the Bel-Del lobbied for the cessation of passenger service. On October 25, 1960, the final train departed for Phillipsburg from Trenton. Freight traffic had remained a viable business for some time; however, during the 1950s, federally funded highway projects enabled material to be hauled by trucks. A gradual reduction of rail usage ensued. Finally, in 1980, the tracks to Raven Rock were removed.

The Bel-Del was considered by many to be the most scenic railroad on the East Coast. Today, its bed remains in use as the D&R Canal Trail, attracting hikers and bicycle traffic. Seventy-seven miles of recreational trail transverses three counties, making it the largest completed course in New Jersey. On weekends, the Belvidere & Delaware River Railway runs tourist steam train excursions between Phillipsburg and Carpentersville using the original Bel-Del layout with vintage equipment.

Houses "Under the Rocks"

Marilyn Cummings

A charming quote has been handed down through the generations regarding a son of the founding family of Raven Rock and referencing his second wife: "When Moses [Quinby] married Hannah Good [in 1801], he took her to live in a little house at the bottom of the hill called 'under the Rocks.'"

Perhaps that quote is more poetic than factual; nonetheless, it could easily be said that it distills the very essence of the dozen or so delightful houses that dot the village and the beautiful setting in which they are located.

Whether the origins of the name Raven Rock came from the birds that still soar overhead, and whether the "riven" rock was formed for the unintended and unimagined future purpose of sheltering small houses at its base, it remains the most captivating of places. Fortunately, for all of us, "the Rocks" have held these little houses under their protection for the better part of two hundred years.

The Setting

Today, Raven Rock is traversed from south to north by Route 29 and is intersected at its center by Quarry Road, winding down rather steeply from the cliffs and, in the process, rather precariously skirting the edge of the quarries before meeting the little valley and Bull's Island at its base. If one is afoot, the village can be best observed from the island's canal path, rather than venturing onto the highway. (Walking the village itself is indeed a bit dangerous, as Route 29 has just become a National Scenic Byway with an ever-increasing amount of traffic. It also must be emphasized here that all of the structures are private dwellings, so these properties should not be trespassed.)

But the setting was not always quite so. The old Lenape Indian path certainly would have followed the edge of the river, but it probably hung closer to the cliffs than does today's road, making the little valley itself wider and more useful than it now is. Old maps show us much about how Raven Rock must have looked before a canal, a railroad and a major highway disturbed its tranquility and devoured its small dirt road. Gardens grew on the riverside of that little road; barns and several houses were located there. At the south end, opposite the various locations of the village store and post office, the several mills and millraces must have operated noisily, replaced eventually by the relative calm of the canal and its lock, finally succeeded by another disquieting era with a station stop for a busy railroad. What there was of a road in the 1800s swung itself close to the string of houses, northward the long way 'round to Frenchtown, past a beautiful stone arched bridge (still standing) and then up the hill, disappearing into what is now Kingwood Township.

In fairness to the Lenape Indians, we must mention with more than a nod that they were the first recorded people to "build" in the area. But they were, for the most part, transient. Their campsites were temporary and easily disassembled. Although evidence of established villages has been found a few miles to the west at Byram and to the east between Federal Twist and Route 519, there is no record of a permanent Native American settlement at Raven Rock.

And at the north end of the village, more than a little removed from the rest of the buildings, there was, and thankfully still is, the tavern—romantic even in its rather forlorn current state. Some ask, "Why there?"—meaning it was such a remote place in that little dirt road for a tavern—and there is no quick answer. Most probably, it was first a random choice for a house site, and that building simply evolved to become a place for the thirsty and weary. Whatever the reason, there it stands to this day for us to ponder.

The Later People and Their Places

The history of the hamlet itself is, of course, the history of the people who came after the Lenapes and the way those people lived their lives. Indeed, the houses of Raven Rock help tell that story, if we will listen closely and imagine.

Quakers Isaiah and Rachel Quinby came to the upper Delaware River Valley from the southern part of New Jersey in one of the early 1700s migrations north of the "Falls at Trenton" allowed by William Penn. In 1743, when Isaiah and Rachel purchased and occupied their three hundred acres, they became among the earliest settlers in the vicinity. Their land was located mostly high above the Delaware River but included the riven cliffs and tiny sliver of valley that bordered the mighty river. They were the ones, therefore, who became parents to the development of the hamlet that we now know as Raven Rock.

The first Quinbys were, out of absolute necessity, pioneer farmers. Such an occupation was perhaps not what they might have wished for or even imagined, but it became their life assignment by their very place in time. They were quite literally in the wilderness not only of what would become a new country but also a totally unsettled and undeveloped part of that new land.

Their earliest thoughts must have been about building shelters for themselves, their animals and their crops. Log houses were often a substantial temporary solution for the former and were much more widespread in every culture than have been properly credited. Indeed, there was a documented settlement of log homes called "Mingo's Hollow" just a few miles to the east of Raven Rock along the Lockatong Creek that survived into the twentieth century. And, of course, logs of one kind or another were always the material for their barns. Wonderful early barns of both dovetail log construction (few remain) and post-and-beam construction (many still stand) can be seen in much of west-central New Jersey.

There were two pressing needs at that point for the housing of settlers: lumber and stoneworkers. Mills sprang up to fill the first need, but probably not in time for the original Quinby house. There was not a sawmill in Raven Rock until the later 1700s. This meant that all timber for construction purposes had to be hand-hewn, a difficult and labor-intensive job. As for stonemasons, there were few in the 1740s. Some were itinerant, covering a wide radius in their quest for employment. But in the later eigtheenth century, a surprising number were local to the surrounding area. It was a skill that was much needed in a place that provided an abundance of lovely, sturdy stone for building purposes.

"THE OLD STONE MANSION"

The original circa 1743 Quinby house undoubtedly was built in the center of their three hundred acres. It is possible that it was made of logs, but no written account of that exists. If the late 1800s photo in this section tells the proper tale, the oldest section of their permanent house appears to be a one-and-a-half-story, one-room structure, probably with a loft, and made of stone (as are the few others of that early time remaining in the area). It was likely constructed entirely by hand without the aid of a sawmill. The stonework looks to have been done by a fairly skilled mason, probably still a roving one at that early time. For their earliest years on the land, that small structure housed Isaiah, Rachel and at least the first several of the thirteen children who were born to them over almost a quarter century.

The current complex of house and farm buildings (now aptly called "Stone Rows Farm"), still sitting high over the Delaware Valley and in the center of what became a great meadow, is surrounded on the south and west by forest and on the east by rows of stone fencing gathered from the fields. Sadly, the original eighteenth-century section of the house apparently was dismantled in the 1930s, and those materials were used to construct an equivalent modern extension (probably on the original foundation) at the back of the remaining house. That second house, which became their primary residence, was probably built in the later 1700s or early 1800s. Isaiah would have been in his seventies or eighties by then, so one or more of his sons most likely had it built for the Quinby family.

In its original form, this second house had two rooms downstairs and two bedchambers up in classic "hall and parlor" configuration, with separate front doors to the right (hall/kitchen) and left (parlor). The long-standing custom of two front doors was to separate the mundane chores (kitchen duties) from the formal ones (receiving guests).

Cooking hearth in the Isaiah Quinby farmstead. This huge fireplace contains one of the most remarkable beehive ovens remaining in the area. Unlike most of these ovens lost from the ravages of weather, this one was protected by a lean-to stone shed. Bedchambers upstairs were likely accessed by a staircase that wound around the hearth, thus the term "winder" (also called "Jersey winder" or "pie stairs"). *Photo by Marilyn Cummings.*

This kitchen retains its huge cooking hearth fireplace and one of the most remarkable "beehive" ovens (so named because if its external shape) remaining in the area. Unlike most of these ovens lost to us from the ravages of weather, this one was protected from an early point by a lean-to stone shed. The bedchambers above were likely accessed by a staircase that wound around the hearth fireplace, thus the term "winder" (also called "Jersey winder" or "pie stairs"). The raised paneling that remains around two of the downstairs fireplaces tells of that early time. Nostalgically, one of those has initials and a date, "W.S. 1799," carved into the mantel molding. The one-room, two-story extension now existing on the left front of this house was probably also constructed in the 1930s remodel.

A most remarkable stone and frame barn still stands sentinel at the entrance to the house complex. This four-bay barn measures twenty-eight by forty-eight feet and includes several slightly later additions, as well as a perpendicular extension on one end, originally open, that was probably a hovel area for animals. Given late eighteenth-century/

The stone and frame Quinby barn as it stands today. *Photo by Marilyn Cummings.*

early nineteenth-century framework, chances are good that father Isaiah watched it being erected in his lifetime.

At Isaiah's death in 1807, his son James received the house and the 225 acres of land that remained (the other 75 acres had gone several years earlier to son Moses). According to Isaiah's will, his third wife (Miriam) was to share the use of house with James during her widowhood. She lived there until her death in 1811. After several centuries of service to the family, locals fondly knew the Quinby house as "the old stone mansion."

In a commemorative poem written about Isaiah Quinby almost one hundred years after his death, he was described as "hard working, patient, plain of dress and humble." In different context, those same words could be applied to the house that they built. If you close your eyes, this verbal snapshot from part of that poem immediately springs to life:

The big fireplace, well kept and clean, where polished trammels hung,
With iron crane above them all on which the kettles swung.
The tongs and shovel leaning stood, bright monuments of pride.
With bellows too in easy reach, near hanging by their side.
The beer jugs warming on the hearth, stood foaming at their tops,
And giving forth a pleasant smell of ginger root and hops.
The earthen bowls, and leaden spoons, with wooden handled knives

And burnished plates of pewter ware, the pride of country wives,
Were leaning forward on the shelves, behind the bars of wood,
Along the open dresser's front, in grand array they stood.

This absolutely endearing scene was no doubt repeated in countless households from the beginning of civilized Old World societies well into the 1800s here in America.

Over time, other structures were added to the Quinby property. On a 1785 map, surveyor Reading Howell marked the existence of a small, square building simply labeled "Quimby." It appears to be in the valley rather than above it, but it is difficult to assess exactly where and what that structure might be. It would have been logical for Howell to identify a building that served a public purpose, such as a tavern. But it has recently been proven that the place later called Saxtonville Tavern was not in existence at that time. Perhaps it was an earlier version of the Quinby store.

THE EARLY 1800S

In December 1801, seventy-five acres of Isaiah's land, including all of the little valley below the cliff, became the property of son Moses. This coincided with the date of Moses's second marriage. In the deed, the land was described "with all and singular the houses, outhouses, stables, etc." So there apparently were two of each identified structure types on that part of the Quinby land, all of which could have been located above the cliff—or very possibly in the valley below. That is part of the mystery surrounding these houses that needed to be unraveled.

The five oldest structures remaining in the village today, parts of which probably date to the late eighteenth or very early nineteenth centuries, are the Saxtonville Tavern at the north end, the Hunt-Reading-Sorby House and Saxton-Heath House in the middle of the village and the Dilts Tenant Cottage and Rodman-Laszlo House at the east end of the village. Several of these structures in their earliest form and location could conceivably have been a candidate for the 1785 Reading Howell map. The northern three of them were within the seventy-five acres that Moses acquired in 1801, and all five houses are equally fascinating studies in the early domestic architecture of the region.

Saxtonville Tavern

Folklore has long associated Moses Quinby, son of the founding family, with the earliest use of this building as a tavern. The 1782 date was also the year of his first marriage, so this use seems logical. But no record is shown of Quinby operating a tavern then or at any other point in time. It is known, however, that he was a storekeeper for a short while in the early 1800s. This would have been after he married his second wife, Hannah, and would also coincide more closely with the actual physical date of this building. If indeed he took Hannah to "live in a little house at the bottom of the hill," that poetic statement could then have been referring to the earliest part of this structure. It's hard to picture, though, that the dozen children he brought to that second marriage would have fit into this little house (see photo on page 49).

The remains of a small stone building to the left of the tavern could possibly have housed his store. When Nathaniel Saxton bought this property from Quinby in 1810, the deed noted, "with all and singular the building and improvements." So a store could have been operating from here in the years before that point, but the house did not function as a tavern until the 1830s. After the succession of tavern owners and tavernkeepers through the 1860s, the McAloan family of Kingwood Township bought the property in 1874, and it remained their family residence for more than 125 years before being sold to the State of New Jersey Green Acres Program in 2007.

The tavern was built in four phases. The early 1800s section was a single-room kitchen with a huge cooking hearth fireplace and a single bedchamber above, accessed by a winder staircase. Because this structure backed up to the cliff behind, a bridge was constructed from the original bedchamber to the upper part of the cliff that may have provided the convenience of a very accessible outhouse. A shed-roof larder or pantry was added to these rooms shortly afterward.

The most remarkable feature of the house at that point was the "summer kitchen," common during the eighteenth and nineteenth centuries with houses of stature and functioning in the hot weather as implied. It can still be seen, located on the front-right side of the house, and is remarkably intact, though without its earlier wooden enclosure. That exterior fireplace repeated a charming feature of the interior-cooking fireplace: a classic bracketed mantel shelf. The two successive additions to the left provided a second room

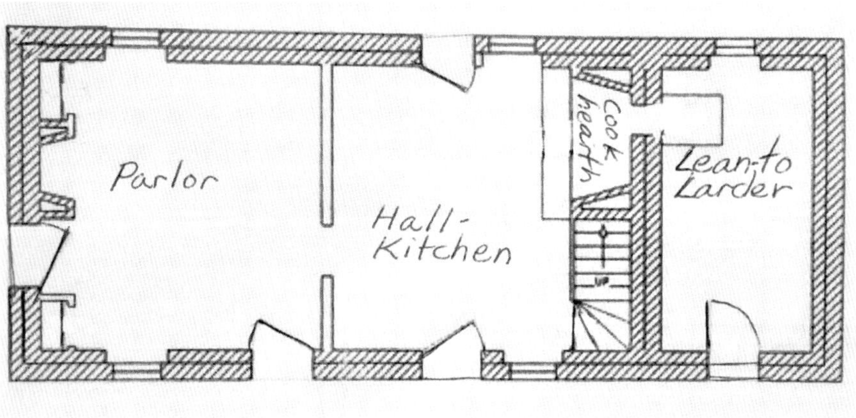

Late eighteenth- and early nineteenth-century house plans were quite simple in design and varied with the wealth of their owners. Poorer families might have only one room downstairs, "the hall" (or kitchen) and one bedchamber upstairs. Adding a parlor (with another bedchamber above), a larder for kitchen storage or even a summer kitchen were measures of status. *Drawn by Marilyn Cummings.*

down and up (circa 1820s) and, in the 1830s, a room down with hall and stairs and three small rooms above. A dramatic second-floor gallery porch was added at that point, but unfortunately it was removed in 1959 as a result of highway improvements. One can clearly imagine this building complex functioning as a tavern and inn, down to the coat pegs that still hang on the hall wall opposite the stairs.

Hunt-Reading-Sorby House

Built in at least three different stages (proceeding from right to left), this is a wonderfully early and unusual house. In fact, it probably is the earliest of the five houses—certainly a contender for the structure shown on the Howell map. It has its kitchen with separate entry door (right), a classic stone-floored cooking hearth with bracketed mantel shelf and the remains of its beehive oven. It also has several winder staircases, one of which is in a unique (and probably later) location across the back of the center entry section, opposite the main door.

On the second floor, the room over the kitchen has one of the most beautiful and original paneled fireplace walls still in existence in the area, with its raised-panel doors and decorative fireplace surround. This wall

Hunt-Reading-Sorby House (the "house under the Rocks") on the left and the Heath-Updegrove House on the right. *Courtesy of Luverne Updegrove Caulton.*

of early woodwork was either never painted or lost its paint so long ago that the wood has aged to a rich dark brown with lovely patina. On the exterior, the two charming arched dormers of the right-hand section were probably added in the later 1800s, and the dormer over the one-and-a-half-story section is a twentieth-century feature. The far left section is late twentieth century, replacing an earlier lean-to shed.

Saxton-Heath House

The original part of this house was probably in existence when Moses acquired his father's land. Could this have been his "little house under the Rocks"? Possibly, but he sold this house just three years later, keeping the tavern house a much longer time. Successive owners of any duration were Jacob Hunt in 1806, Nathaniel Saxton in 1810 and Peter Dilts from 1819 to 1839. The house then came into the Elijah Heath family from 1839 to 1867 and was where renter George Huffman operated a general store and post office through the mid-1800s.

The timeline for the three parts of this house is curious. The stone section (left side) is very early (probably turn of the 1800s), which probably puts it slightly earlier than Saxtonville Tavern, but it still is less of a contender for the Howell map. It has a similar and equally amazing summer kitchen, this one being totally separate from the main structure. The interior of the stone house is remarkably formal, with detailed mantels, raised-panel doors and classic moldings. The room divisions of this structure make it quite elegant and private for such a small early house. It is hard to imagine that Quinby would have operated a business here; it is far more likely that the wealthiest man in the village, Nathaniel Saxton, made this his home at least for a time. The other two sections of this house were built several decades later.

Rodman-Laszlo Farmstead

Fronted by carriage houses and flanked in back by the old farmstead barn (converted to a charming home), this is the last house on Quarry Road as one climbs the hill out of Raven Rock. It has an early 1800s banked (built into the hill) "cellar kitchen," not uncommon in the

Rodman-Laszlo farmstead on Quarry Road. *Photo by R. Curt Chinnici.*

general area and certainly not surprising in this situation, considering that the rock forms the base for all of the structures here. It houses a classic cooking fireplace with stone hearth, a simple mantel shelf identical to others in the vicinity and heavy hewn ceiling beams. A trio of winder staircases, ubiquitous to this early period (and found in a much wider area than just New Jersey), ascend in a dizzying spiral from cellar to attic with an unusual built-in handrail to aid in climbing each successive level.

The eastern half of the house was constructed in two phases at a slightly later point in time, though not by much, as the parlor (center) has a lovely early 1800s fireplace overmantel, with dentil and punch-gouged detail, as well as a built-in china cabinet. Doors in this section are the raised four-panel type rather than the common six-panel, and these are seldom seen in this early construction. As the house evolved over time, the kitchen was moved from the banked cellar area to the far right side of the second floor. Earlier photos show a porch roof over the two road-facing cellar doors. But the most inexplicable feature of this later section is that there apparently was never a front entry; access is only from the banked second-floor rear of the house.

Dilts Tenant Cottage

The age on this small gem is a bit hard to decipher. The original section (probably circa 1800–1820) was constructed of stone, only one room deep with no evidence of a stairway to access the second floor, even though there is a bedchamber above. It had a fairly substantial stone fireplace and chimney (both recently replaced) that would have cooked and warmed sufficiently for this singular purpose. The ceiling beams in this room are lovely; they were meant to be exposed and show great early paint history. Partially visible to the left, the two-story frame section (one room down and one up) was added at a slightly later point, though not by much as the rafter history for both sections is similar. This section boasts one of the tiniest cellars on record—just big enough to turn around in.

The one-story, wraparound wing to the far left and the lean-to shed on the right were later still, probably early twentieth century. In recent times, the stucco has been removed from the exterior façade. (This is a trend of

Dilts Tenant Cottage. This famous house is clearly depicted in the background of the painter Daniel Garber's masterpiece, *Our Country Neighbors. Photo by R. Curt Chinnici.*

recent years, as people have wanted to show the stonework underneath.) Scant references available describe a "tenement house" in the vicinity, and this may be the structure to which they were referring.

OUTLYING LANDS AND LATER TIMES

On the outskirts of the village are locations significant to the history of the immediate area.

The Ferry House

A very early inland route to the Delaware River just east of Raven Rock, aptly called Ferry Road in the 1700s, now goes by the name Federal Twist. A ferry was operated at the terminus of this road from the early 1700s. Such transports were usually identified by the name of their owner and changed names often over the next century. Thus, it first was Rose's Ferry, established by the Rose family who owned land on both sides of the river. On the New Jersey side, it subsequently became McClain's, then Thorne's, then for many years Painter's Ferry and ultimately, in the early 1800s, Johnson's Ferry (first named for Martin Johnson and then for a succession of other family members; see photo on page 39).

In the 1820s, as a logical extension to their ferry business, the Johnson family began operating a tavern or public house. The inn was eventually enlarged and apparently came to occupy a prominent position in the business and social life of the Raven Rock community. Recognized as a place of public assembly, it accommodated its patrons by including large second-floor rooms for meetings. It is shown on the 1851 Cornell map as the "W. Johnson Hotel" and, shortly after that time, became the private residence of the Huffman family.

The structure itself appears to have started out as one room and is described in a 1950 auction advertisement as having "a kitchen wing with a large open hearth fireplace." This would undoubtedly have been the small room at the back of the house. The early 1800s enlargement was "a central block, 2½ stories in height, containing eight rooms with a wide central hall." This much larger structure faced toward the river road. The ad further describes the very much intact "adjacent tap room still retaining its old bottle cabinets." In preparation for the widening of Route 29, the building went to auction as described. But with no buyer stepping forward to rescue it, sadly, it was torn down.

Also on Federal Twist Road, up from the ferry landing, the Johnson family developed two farm complexes (including lovely mid-nineteenth-century barns) early in their history there. The houses sit across the road from each other like the cousins they must have always been, high on the hill and safely up from the river flooding that occasionally occurs. Facing south, they both enjoy beautiful views of the little valley below.

VanCamp-Johnson-Shuck House

The ell-shaped stone house to the west is the earlier of the two homes. From the exterior, it looks like a rather simple assemblage, and three distinct stone sections vie for attention. But one look in the cellar tells quite a different tale. Under the elbow of the ell, there is clear evidence of an eighteenth-century structure that, over time, has been much rearranged. On the first floor above this area is an early corner fireplace, and without doubt, it was flanked by a winder staircase to its left side (now gone). Several other winders in the house have also been removed, added or rearranged, but the south wing (circa 1840) has been kept totally intact. The remaining (but perhaps not the first) cooking hearth fireplace is located in west wing (circa 1800–1820), complete with its beehive oven that appears to have remained in use into the twentieth century, as well as a charming assortment of storage cabinets recessed into the walls of the room.

An 1885 sales advertisement implies that this structure may have functioned as a two-family house earlier in its history, and indeed, the upstairs division of rooms does offer numerous bedchambers. It also boasted one of the first bathrooms in the area that until very recently had its tin tub with wooden surround still in place. Water was pumped from a windmill located halfway between the house and the springhouse to one of the sheds formerly above the house and then gravity-fed to the second floor in order to operate that amazing new room.

Johnson Springhouse

An absolutely remarkable, one-of-a-kind stone outbuilding below the older house combined the most amazing assortment of functions. It was first and foremost a springhouse, fed from a continuously flowing underground water source; it provided water to both houses until recently. However, it was far more than that. In earlier times, it was also a summer

VanCamp-Johnson-Schuck farmstead springhouse on Federal Twist Road. This is a unique multipurpose building that was used for a smokehouse, a washhouse, a servant's quarter and for keeping perishables cool. *Photo by Marilyn Cummings.*

kitchen with a large cooking hearth fireplace, as well as a smokehouse, with its charred beams still supporting lag poles. The springhouse was no doubt an occasional sleeping quarter for a hired hand (the shadow of a loft area still apparent). A water trough chilling area around the perimeter was for milk and the like, and in recent memory, it was the family "wash house," with a large stone drain still intact on its south side.

Johnson-Emmons House

The more linear house to the east tells of a slightly later time. What is now its center section (early 1800s) was most probably the original part of the house, the cellar of which was excavated long after the house was built (not uncommon and always an amazing feat). This section had a cooking hearth fireplace (remaining), a winder staircase tucked in the front corner (removed) and hints of a one-story gabled room to the right of the kitchen. That room, which may have been a larder or summer kitchen, was subsequently replaced with a lean-to shed, which evolved into the working kitchen when cookstoves came into use. A hand pump, which brought water to a dry sink, still retains its place of honor in that area.

The left section of the house, a decade or two younger though still with hewn cellar beams, had a side hall and formal parlor with a much smaller fireplace, drawers tucked into the aprons of the windows and winder staircases to the cellar (removed) and attic (remaining). A front bay extension was added during Victorian times, and the enlargement to the right of that was done in the late twentieth century.

Hankinson-Huffman House

The Hankinson family first owned this property on Route 29, east of the ferry crossing, in the 1700s. The Huffman-Hoffman family then owned it for more than a century. For the last several decades of the 1900s, it was known as the "Doll House," referring to the Karsan store that sold antiques and an extensive collection of miniature dollhouse items. It is also located next to the Lockatong Creek Bridge. The house that stands here today is composed of an early 1800s section (center), with a narrow two-story addition of slightly later vintage (right), and a mid-1800s addition (left). Each section has lovely, intact features and details indicative of those respective periods. However, a study of the cellar area reveals a surprising configuration that suggests an earlier structure. The left cellar section has the stone remains of back-to-back corner fireplace supports and was built as an entirely separate structure from the center section (i.e., four independent foundation walls). This fact, plus the heavy hewn beams in this part of the cellar, further suggests an eighteenth-century date for the original structure. The farmstead has the remains of several interesting outbuildings, including a summer kitchen.

THE 1830S AND 1840S

It is easy to understand that this period, with the building of the Delaware & Raritan Canal, was a time of prosperity for the village. The recently established tavern was expanded to accommodate the needs of the village workers and travelers alike. For the houses of Raven Rock, this was a transition time that was stunning in several ways. For the first time in the history of the world, stoves (for both cooking and heating) were replacing the cooking hearths that had served mankind almost since the beginning of time. Fireplaces during this period were first reduced in size and then eventually eliminated. Chimneys became much smaller because they were needed only to vent those revolutionary new stoves. The winder staircases that had served early houses so well no longer wound around the fireplace. However, winders didn't just suddenly disappear; they were simply moved to more convenient locations. And rooms in their layout and function became more specialized, particularly the kitchen.

McAlone House

This house is older than it might appear at first glance, probably dating fairly early in the 1800s. In the 1980s, it underwent a transformation of sorts. A small front porch and shed were removed, and a layer of stone was applied to the façade. What is even more telling is that a substantial interior chimney in the left gable was removed. And on the inside, along with the removal of the fireplace, a tiny kitchen was built in place of the winder staircase. But clues in the attic, including pegged rafter joinings and very wide attic floorboards, tell a story of slightly greater age. Small and simply detailed, it was probably first built for someone associated with the canal during that boom time.

Heath-Huffman Store

This structure, incorporating a first-floor store, was built close to the eighteenth-century Saxton-Heath House (aforementioned). This circa 1830s building can easily be pictured as the store and post office that it was, with a stone fireplace to warm the customers or to sit beside and catch up on local gossip. Sufficient living quarters above served the merchant's family, and a very utilitarian cellar had direct front access. Also within this time period, these two buildings were joined together by a third section, resulting in the absolutely charming trio of buildings you see there today (see photo on page 38).

Lake-Colligan House

Lake-Colligan House. *Photo by R. Curt Chinnici.*

The most well-known owners of this house were the Colligan family of the later 1800s, famous for their Colligan Inn in neighboring Stockton (now the Stockton Inn). Although there was some evidence of an earlier configuration of the main section (now removed), this structure from style and detail standpoints falls closer to the time period of circa 1840–60. The right-hand section is earlier than the left. Exterior additions include a later decorative

Victorian porch covering a simple mid-century façade, as well as a sympathetic twenty-first-century addition on the left. The interior of the earlier section has a fireplace with a lovely mantel and plastered overmantel. It also boasts elements that would have been innovative for their time: both a built-in second-floor closet and beam supports that include struts and cross bracing, unusual in houses of this vintage.

Feeney and Opdyke Houses

These two houses sit side by side, almost like siblings, with one foot in the past and one in the future. Like their earlier Raven Rock neighbors, they are built up rather than out. Each of these houses was essentially a three-story structure, tall and slim, with its back to the sheltering rock cliff. Their first floors are stone; the second and third floors are frame. Surprisingly, they both retain the early construction technique of heavy pegged window frames. Yet, at the same time, they were houses no longer served by large fireplaces, with stoves and flues taking their place within small fireplace openings. Both had parlors on the left and kitchens on the right. Each had more defined sleeping rooms but retained the

Johnson-Feeney House. The large porch is a twentieth-century addition. *Photo by R. Curt Chinnici.*

Winder stairs in the Johnson-Feeney House. *Photo by R. Curt Chinnici.*

winder staircases in corner locations. Both added stone lean-tos on the right shortly after they were built, for cooking use. Wesley Johnson, the postmaster for Raven Rock in the 1860s, once owned the Feeney House. He died while waiting for the mail that he was to carry across the bridge to Lumberville. The Opdyke House was the location of a blacksmith shop that repaired rails for the railroad and a common water source that has been shared by several of the neighbors for generations.

Williamson House

Clearly a product of the mid-1800s timeframe, this house has no evidence of fireplaces. Instead, small chimney flues served both downstairs rooms. One room was a parlor (left) and the other room a kitchen (right). A center stairway accesses the two upstairs bedchambers that were probably unheated, as evidenced by grates in the upstairs floors that would have transferred stove or furnace heat from below. A twentieth-century lean-to was added to the back of the house, and the kitchen was moved there to enjoy the incredible drama of the cliff behind. In the late twentieth century, the entire house was stuccoed over its original frame construction, at which time some of its door and window openings were rearranged and the porch removed. The grounds include a delightful root cellar to the left of the house.

Johnson Tenant House

This house (circa 1840–60), with its two rooms down, two rooms up and center staircase, retains some of its four-panel doors, beaded trim and box locks indicative of the mid-1800s period. For much of its life, it served as a tenant house for the Johnson farms on Federal Twist Road. Its history includes a remarkable feet-per-day move in the early 1950s to save it from the widening of Route 29. In 2005, it was doubled in size with the addition on the right, and a charming pent roof was added to the resulting façade (see photo on page 150).

THE 1850S AND 1860S

This era, with the coming of the railroad, was an equally prosperous time for the Raven Rock villagers. Imagine the initial excitement of the huge steam locomotives pulling into the little hamlet and whistling their arrival for all to hear. It was quite a contrast from the serenity of the canal. But as far as houses go, this was more a time of houses lost than houses gained.

Heath-Updegrove House

This is a much later version (circa 1860s) of a house that kept the classic "hall and parlor" plan with two front doors (still properly separating the family chores from social functions). This house remained in the same family for much of the twentieth century and was passed down to their daughter, Hannah, who lived in it all of her life. According to a close neighbor, "Even late in the twentieth century, the house was pretty original…a Sears refrigerator with round shoulders, oil heater, water pump, etc. The attic thus was a treasure-trove of really old interesting stuff." It was the last dwelling in Raven Rock to keep its outhouse functional.

C.S. Johnson Store

According to several sources, this bungalow was built on the foundation of an earlier structure, probably dating to the mid-1800s. It is shown on the 1873 Beers map as the C.S. Johnson store, also identified by some sources as a post office. A newspaper article noted that "[t]he store building burned down in 1876. A bungalow was built on the same stone foundations by Augustus Reading. Reading later ran a basket factory at the corner of the road leading to the railroad station." This building has undoubtedly served many varied functions over the last 150 years. A beautiful spring cascades down the rock cliff to the left of the house, reassuring owners past and present of the unchanging path of nature in a changing world.

The early deed description for this property (which at that point also included what would become the various parcels of land on either side of

C.S. Johnson Store as it stands today along Quarry Road; evidence of its use as a store are the large windows on the ground level. *Photo by R. Curt Chinnici.*

this structure) is one of the most charming one could happen upon and gives us a reflection of the little village as if looking into the discarded fragment of a mirror. Written on now yellowed paper in the flowing script of old, it reads in part: "Beginning at a stone with coal under, standing on the hill on the northerly side of a wagon way or farm road in a line formerly between lands of Joseph Rodman's and Nathaniel Saxton, thence along said line…"

Times, people and circumstances long gone.

THE LOST HOUSES OF RAVEN ROCK

We would be remiss not to mention the houses of the village that over the centuries have been lost to us for one reason or another.

Quarry Houses

Heartbreaking in their eminent demise, and painted by local artists before they were lost to us, are several mid-1800s houses on the south side of Quarry Road that were literally consumed by the operation of the quarry.

Holcombe-Reading House

North of Saxtonville Tavern, early maps identified a house belonging to J. Holcomb. Noted also as "H. Holcombe" by Sorby, who wrote, "It was adjacent to the tavern, but is now demolished." A.B. Reading is shown as the owner on the 1873 *Beers Atlas*. It was lost sometime between the late 1800s and mid-1900s.

Welch-Emmons House

When the extension of Route 29 was carved through the little village in the late 1950s, this house, built between 1874 and 1884, was demolished. It was located to the right of the Lake-Colligan House and had lovely gardens and a larger block of land with it than most of the others did. Much to the dismay of the village residents, the family sold their house and property to the state highway department. Tourists came to see the gardens and giant wisteria vines.

Bull's Island

Mention is also made of several houses located on Bull's Island for which no documentary photographs can be found—only vague references to several early dwellings next to the mills, as well as another that noted, "the August Herholz house that sustained flood damage in 1955." Several people who worked on the island tell of early twentieth-century cottages (rented for use in the summer) that are now gone, victims of the relentless floods.

The Pie House

By far, the most captivating story about a structure long lost is that which the locals called the "Pie House." Aside from the dwellings associated with the mills, it was the only house known to be located on the river side of the little dirt road. The owner appears on the 1851 Cornell map and the 1873 Beers map as A. (Ashbel) Welch. According to the legend, that stone house suddenly found itself located so close to the newly built railroad that the engineers on the trains could reach out from their cabs

A 1904 Oldsmobile owned by George Green and parked in front of Barbara Coar's house during the Missing Link Art Show in 1958. This vehicle was destroyed and rebuilt by George Green after a car accident that inspired the law requiring cars to maintain a minimum speed on the Pennsylvania Turnpike. It took first prize (a gold Oldsmobile) at the Automobile Golden Jubilee in 1946. In the early '70s, George could still be seen in Lambertville cranking his old Olds. *Courtesy of Luverne Updegrove Caulton.*

to the windowsill of the house, where freshly baked pies were cooling… and they would logically help themselves. Whether exaggerated or not, it makes a great story. The house was said to have burned down in 1874. What a loss to the village, the railroad and especially to the engineers.

Sturdy houses all, like the people who built them. One of the most remarkable footnotes about these treasured places is that many of them have stayed either in the same family or under the same continuous ownership for long periods of time. Equally amazing, large parcels of the land around the little village have also remained intact, some almost from the inception of the early land divisions. Many of the inhabitants of these historic dwellings seem to know that they are merely temporary stewards in a much larger swath of time. Preservation here has come to mean not only the land itself but also the buildings connected to this land. Generations yet to come, therefore, will owe to the village and surrounding area that same dedication to preservation and protection.

THE ARTISTS COME TO RAVEN ROCK

R. Curt Chinnici

Raven Rock has been the inspiration for numerous works of art for more than 140 years. Artists have fallen for its striking beauty and its unique location along the Delaware River. Because the town faces south, the light that falls on the houses and quarry walls of this place is strong. This gives the viewer lots of opportunities throughout the day to paint. Because the village is in its own narrow valley, the morning mist and nearby bodies of water add softness to the atmosphere, making Raven Rock an ideal place for landscape painting.

The first artist to illustrate the natural marvel of the Raven Rock, the stone palisade that has the large vertical split, was Augustus Köllner in 1873. Köllner immigrated to Philadelphia from Germany and illustrated a book called *Views of American Cities*. His watercolor and lithography work was exhibited at the Pennsylvania Academy of Fine Art (PAFA) in the 1860s, and his success was due to the fact that he illustrated natural views of the Delaware River and New Jersey. He drew a close-up view of the split in the rock face with gentlemen viewing it while standing on the rock. The view is not very realistic since the cliff is relatively sheer and inaccessible to casual climbing. His other view of the rock is wonderful because it shows two of the early houses in the village, people and the road that traveled through the village at the foot of the rock.

During the first half of the twentieth century, Bucks County became a haven for artists and entertainers. Many of them either worked, lived there full time or used the region as a getaway from New York City or Philadelphia. "Weekenders" arrived during the 1920s and '30s. The popularity of the area extended into Hunterdon County and particularly Delaware Township, the home of Raven Rock. Scores of artists, like Daniel Garber and Edward Redfield, painted scenes along the Delaware River and the Delaware Valley to create a legacy of art that came to be known as Pennsylvania impressionism. This first wave arrived at the beginning of the twentieth century. More artists came a generation later and developed impressionism into other forms of painting like realism and abstraction.

The 1950s brought a flurry of art-related activity to Raven Rock. In 1951, a branch of the Charles-Fourth art gallery opened in one of the houses in Raven Rock. Peggy Lewis moved here with her husband, Michael, a fellow artist. The couple rented one of Barbara Coar's three houses under the rock that gives the town its name. Their home was decorated with ultramodern furnishings designed by him, and they featured the artwork of unknown artists in the modern style of painting. After one year, the gallery moved to New Hope, Pennsylvania. The tragic drowning of one of their children's young friends in the canal may have made them nervous about living so close to the river.

One of Raven Rock's most outspoken proponents of the arts was Berthold A. Sorby. He was the librarian at the Hunterdon County Historical Society, and he had worked for the most well-known rare book business in the country, the Rosenbach Company of Philadelphia. His partner in life was Englishman Geoffrey Roberts, a successful businessman in New York. The two moved to Raven Rock in the 1940s, and since they were well off, they traveled to Mexico and Europe in the summers. Their social circle included other prominent gay men who resided nearby, such as the writer Glenway Westcott (a major American novelist during the 1920–40 period and a member of the expatriate literary community in Paris; he was the model for Hemingway's main character in *The Sun Also Rises* and was the older brother of Lloyd Westcott, who donated a large farm as a preserve in Delaware Township) and Monroe Wheeler (co-founder of Harrison of Paris publishing company and a director at the Museum of Modern Art in New York).

Sorby was also good friends with his charming neighbor, Barbara Coar, who joined him in many publicity schemes to promote Raven

Residents Bert Sorby and Barbara Coar posing with a sign for the local newspaper, 1958. *Courtesy of the* Hunterdon Democrat.

Rock. Barbara moved to Raven Rock in 1946 from Chestnut Hill, a tony section of Philadelphia. She lived in one of the most picturesque homes in the village. The house was composed of three attached structures in which she rented two houses to tenants until she passed away in 1973. Barbara was a writer who worked for a national features syndicate. Her heirs sold her home to Robert Goodwin, a designer and interior decorator who recounted many of the stories about Raven Rock to the author. She was a very social person, and everyone within a seven-mile radius knew Miss Barbara Coar.

Barbara Coar and B.A. Sorby were kindred spirits, fond of throwing parties for their artistic friends and promoting the cultural and natural beauty of their village. In 1958, after the State of New Jersey had dragged its feet in completing the highway through Raven Rock for many years, the two friends invented an event to promote the village and draw attention to the deplorable conditions of the road here.

The Missing Link Art Show was conceived in January 1958, and Sorby immediately placed an article in the local paper calling for pictures depicting landmarks in the area of Raven Rock. The two friends figured that the publicity from the show would generate interest in Raven Rock and the deplorable condition of the road here. Sorby already owned the two Köllner images described earlier. For the next several months, the two collected paintings and artwork for the show from friends, strangers and professional contacts. They amassed an impressive group of artwork to exhibit that was on par with any museum show. The exhibit was sponsored by the Citizens Committee for the Completion of Route 29 and was open between May 10 and May 18, 1958. Admission was twenty-five cents, and you could buy a raffle ticket to win a painting by R.A.D. Miller for another quarter. A total of six hundred people attended the show in the house of Barbara Coar, which was actually the former post office.

Congressman William B. Windall attended the show and assured Citizens Committee members that he would pursue federal funds to finish the completion of Route 29. Other prominent attendees were Albert T. Gardner of the Metropolitan Museum of Art and Arthur Miller, the president of the American Watercolor Society. As an added stunt, Sorby's partner, Geoffrey Roberts, dressed up in an ape suit and posed for pictures for the regional newspaper. He did this to illustrate and poke fun at the ridiculousness of the "missing link." One politician of note missing from the show was Governor Meyner, who notoriously diverted funds for road improvements on the Missing Link.

Several paintings by Kenneth Nunamaker and an R.A.D. Miller picture were sold during the show's run. The stained-glass artist Dorothy Larson Hotchkiss sold work to New York collectors. To create some excitement, an original oil painting was offered as a raffle prize. This was R.A.D. Miller's painting *Back of Raven Rock*. Neighbor Anton Schuck won the painting out of 250 people who paid for a chance. His daughter, Rebecca Schuck Davis, now owns this painting.

The regional newspaper at the time advertised another local landmark to visit in addition to the art show: the giant wisteria owned by George Emmons. It covered much of the rock wall known as the Raven Rock, and Mr. Emmons built a large trellis out of wood to support it. The fifty-year-old vine attracted many visitors when it was at its annual peak of flowering in May. The newspaper noted that it was a popular subject for painters and "color film enthusiasts."

So, the people came and the show was a big success, as told by the numerous positive reviews of it in the newspaper. However, the organizers

Betty Schuck Davis holding the R.A.D. Miller painting that her father won in a raffle at the Missing Link Art Show in 1958. The frame is original to the painting, too. *Photo by R. Curt Chinnici.*

Daniel Garber, *Our Country Neighbors*, 1937. The remains of this tree are still there at the base of Quarry Road. *Used with permission of Primrose Press, New Hope, Pennsylvania.*

may not have realized how significant their little show was in the context of art history.

The group of artists whose work was exhibited comprised some of the best American landscape artists from the first half of the twentieth century. The rest of this chapter is an annotated list of the artists and the artwork that were part of the Missing Link Art Show. All of these artists either lived very close to Raven Rock or visited the village to paint. Artwork for many of these artists has seen a sharp increase in public interest and monetary value in the last two decades. Several works have reached six-figure levels at auction. Berthold Sorby typed the list of artwork and artists in the show, but dates and sizes are missing for the work. He sometimes included the name of the owner of the work, which was sometimes more important than the artwork itself. All work is oil on canvas unless noted otherwise.

Ben Badura

Johnson's Farm–Tenant House and *Johnson's Farm Yard at Raven Rock*

Badura lived across the river from Raven Rock in the town of Lumberville, Pennsylvania. He was from Milwaukee but studied painting under Daniel Garber at the Pennsylvania Academy of Fine Arts. He met his wife, Faye Swengel, at school, and soon they moved to Bucks County, Pennsylvania. Badura was also an accomplished picture frame maker, and he made frames for many famous Delaware Valley artists. In addition to painting *Johnson's Farm Yard at Raven Rock*, he painted the quarry at the center of Raven Rock village.

Alexander Farnham

Autumn Smoke—Raven Rock

Farnham was probably the youngest artist in the show. After his service in the U.S. Navy as an illustrator, he made a career as a landscape painter and has exhibited extensively. Farnham has written several books on New Jersey toolmakers, and he still lives close to Raven Rock on a farm.

John Folinsbee

Byram Quarry, from Point Pleasant

Folinsbee moved to New Hope, Pennsylvania, in 1916, and he and his wife, Ruth, founded the Phillips Mill Community Association in 1929. This group still hosts many art events and holds an annual juried art show. Folinsbee painted in a darker palette than most Delaware Valley painters, yet in a realistic style.

Daniel Garber

Country Neighbors, *Johnson's Farm—Raven Rock* and *Emmons Garden*

Garber's work is some of the most celebrated and valuable work of the Pennsylvania impressionists. Garber came from Indiana to study at the Pennsylvania Academy of Fine Arts. He went on to develop a style of impressionism that combines realism with vibrant effects of light and color. Garber established his home in Cuttalossa, near Lumberville, where he painted and created fine prints. He taught many artists during the forty years as an instructor at PAFA. A photo taken of him at the Missing Link show was the last one taken of him before his death at age seventy-eight.

Garber, like Nunamaker to follow, painted Raven Rock often. *Country Neighbors*, from 1937, shows two of the villages small stone houses in the background, covered in stucco and whitewash. Garber's personal notes stated that it was "[p]ainted from what is left, of Raven Rock Station." These same homes appear in his painting *Little Blue Cottage and Others*, from 1928. It includes the tenant farmhouse up on Quarry Road. Garber painted *Emmons Garden* in 1949, and it shows the rust-colored stone of the Lumberville quarries in the distance. It is a blessing that George Emmons's fabulous garden is forever memorialized in Garber's painting since his house and yard were lost when the new highway was put through Raven Rock. Some of his wisteria remains at the foot of the rock today.

ETHEL D. HOFFMAN

Raven Rock—Lumberville Footbridge and *River Road along the Missing Link*

Not much information is available about Ethel Drake Hoffman, except that her paintings are very much in the modern realist tradition of landscape painting, with grayed-out colors and few figures.

DOROTHY HOYT

Under Raven Rock, collection of Mr. and Mrs. Carlton Cooley, Raven Rock, New Jersey

Currently, no information is available about Hoyt. The painting's owner, Carlton Cooley, was a composer and a violist with the Philadelphia Orchestra under conductor Eugene Ormandy. Before joining the Philadelphia Orchestra in 1954, he worked under Arturo Toscanini with the NBC Symphony Orchestra for many years. Cooley and his wife, Ada, resided just north of the Saxtonville Tavern.

AUGUSTUS KÖLLNER

Raven Rock and *Raven Rock Houses*, 1873, watercolors, collection of B.A. Sorby

See the previous description of Köllner's work. These watercolors were owned by Sorby but are now in the possession his partner's heirs.

SIGMUND KOZLOW

Along the Delaware, pastel

Kozlow studied art in New York and then went on to become well known for his scenes of Bucks County and Rockport, Massachusetts. Besides being adept painting landscapes and seascapes, he was also a photographer. He exhibited at PAFA and the Phillips Mill annual exhibitions.

George Laszlo

Raven Rock Bridge and Cove, Bull's Island

George Laszlo was a Hungarian immigrant who made his art career in New York before moving to a large converted barn atop Raven Rock with his wife, Edna Laszlo. The two of them added greatly to the social scene in Raven Rock. Edna was previously married to the painter and color theorist Maitland Graves. Their son, John Maitland Graves, was also an artist who worked for years in Raven Rock. George Laszlo patented a simple intaglio printing press that he sold through a family business called Rembrandt Graphic Art. This operation was located in Raven Rock before moving in 1975 to Rosemont, New Jersey, just a few miles away. Edna also was a painter and won awards at Phillips Mill Shows. Edna established the George Laszlo Print Award at Phillips Mill for excellent work in the area of printmaking. George was also a prolific printer and painter.

Dr. W.W. McNeary

Up River from Lumberville Bridge and *Canal Lock Keeper's House*

Dr. McNeary lived in Lumberville next to Fern Coppedge and had retired from the Philadelphia College of Pharmacy. He enjoyed painting Delaware River views.

Anne Steele Marsh

Portland-Columbia Bridge

Ms. Marsh studied at the Cooper Union Art School in New York, and her work is in many collections, including the Metropolitan Museum of Art and the Museum of Modern Art (MoMA). She and her husband founded the Hunterdon Art Center in Clinton, New Jersey.

R.A.D. MILLER

Rosemont Hill, *Raven Rock* and *Back of Raven Rock* (raffle prize)

Robert Alexander Darrah Miller studied at PAFA with Daniel Garber and painted in the traditional styles of American regionalism and realism. Miller moved from Chestnut Hill, Philadelphia, to Bucks County in 1928. Miller lived in Lumberville, Pennsylvania, and there he had several unsettling experiences with ghosts at the house he rented with a fellow artist. He then married Celia Belden Marshall, the daughter of the former owner of Phillips Mill. Miller went on to paint in a more modern style in the 1930s and painted charming mural panels of local scenes for the Stockton Inn in 1936. He had gained experience in mural work by working on a mural project under his friend Thomas Hart Benton in 1932.

Miller made his living with commissioned portraits, yet he was also accomplished in the genre of landscape painting. He also sailed in the Caribbean, designed jewelry and clothing and became a skilled carpenter. His wife died in 1953, and R.A.D. supposedly painted less and was depressed for the last decade of his life. Eventually, Miller became involved with Barbara Coar of Raven Rock, who lived directly across the pedestrian bridge. He painted several pictures in Raven Rock, and the current owners of Barbara Coar's house have found a wooden board with the carving "RAD + BC" in the walls of their historic home. Miller helped Coar and Sorby with the Missing Link Art Show by painting a smaller version of a painting he had previously made of Raven Rock. This painting is ten inches by fourteen inches in size and has notes on the back indicating that it is a "rush" job and the name of the person ordering it, "Coar." Sadly, R.A.D. Miller took his own life on December 22, 1966, at his wife's grave site.

BEVERIDGE MOORE

Across the River from Raven Rock

Mr. Moore was a nationally recognized artist from Richmond, Virginia, who made his home in Doylestown, Pennsylvania. His work combines figurative and landscape elements in paintings that evoke expressive moods.

KENNETH R. NUNAMAKER

Autumn Leaves, Rosemont Road, The Boat Makers House, Hillside Houses Raven Rock, John's Garden Wall, John's House, Raven Rock, River Road, Raven Rock, Saxtonville Tavern–Spring and *Saxtonville Tavern–Winter*

Kenneth Nunamaker was a self-taught artist from Akron, Ohio, yet made a living in the printing industry. He moved to Philadelphia in

"RIVER ROAD, RAVEN ROCK" *by* K. R. NUNAMAKER

PAINTINGS

BY PROMINENT DELAWARE VALLEY ARTISTS

GARBER, REDFIELD, NUNAMAKER, BADURA, WIESE,
SWENGLE, MILLER, KOLLNER, LASZLO AND OTHERS

Scenes Along the "Missing Link", near Raven Rock

to be held

IN THE OLD POST OFFICE, Raven Rock, N. J.

Three Miles North of Stockton, N. J.
on the *"Missing Link"* of Route 29
Across the Foot Bridge from the Black Bass Hotel, Lumberville, Penna.

May 10 through May 18

HOURS: EVERY DAY INCLUDING
SATURDAY AND SUNDAY, 12-6

ADMISSION, 25 CENTS

A 1958 program for Missing Link Art Show, *Courtesy of Betty Schuck Davis.*

1918 but then bought a home in Centre Bridge, Pennsylvania, in 1923 and lived there until his death in 1957. His famous neighbor, Edward Redfield, influenced "Nuny." His son, Alfred, was a partner in his commercial art studio from 1945 to 1957, and both painted scenes around Raven Rock. Kenneth had the most work of any artist in the Missing Link Art Show, and the exhibit was a tribute to the artist, who had just passed away the previous year. Nunamaker used lots of paint called impasto in his landscapes. His pictures of Raven Rock houses typically have no human figures and show the homes in their rustic state. He was fond of using chromatic grays, or colors made from mixing opposite colors together.

Edward Redfield

Calling for the Mail–Raven Rock Post Office, collection of Arthur M. Eastburn

Redfield is one of the most celebrated of the New Hope School of painters. He painted en plein air, or outside, during all kinds of weather on usually large canvases. Redfield was fourteen years old when he moved to the area in 1912, camping on an island in the river across from the Burgess-Lea Farm. He would eventually establish his home and studio in Centre Bridge, Pennsylvania, across the Delaware River from Stockton, New Jersey. Redfield was eighty-nine during the Missing Link show, yet he still sent a painting to the committee for inclusion in the exhibit. Redfield stopped painting in the 1940s and produced hooked rugs and painted furniture pieces until his death in 1965.

George Remailly

Spring Thaw

At this time, no information is available.

CLAIRE RUSSELL

The Garden Gate, Raven Rock, collection of Miss Barbara Coar

Ms. Russell lived in Christiansted, United States Virgin Islands, and owned the Reef and Sand and Crown House in Frederiksted. Like her friend Barbara Coar, she was also prone to car accidents and flipped her car over when she struck a tree on St. Croix in 1964.

ALBERT SCHUMACHER

Valley Village, Raven Rock, collection of Mr. and Mrs. Kenyon Nicholson, Raven Rock, New Jersey

No information is available about the artist, but the owner, Kenyon Nicholson, was a playwright and screenwriter who had a farm very close to Raven Rock. He wrote for Broadway, radio and several motion picture studios in Hollywood. Nicholson wrote several films for Joan Crawford, and he was an early director of the Bucks County Playhouse with Moss Hart. He eventually opened a bookstore that has become Farley's Bookshop in New Hope, Pennsylvania.

GEORGE SOTTER

Road to Raven Rock—Moonlight, collection of Mrs. G. Sotter

George Sotter was a well-known landscape painter and a designer of stained-glass windows. He was fond of depicting winter scenes in moonlight, thus the view of Raven Rock in the evening. He studied under the famous impressionist painter Edward Redfield but made a career designing and running a workshop that produced high-quality stained-glass work.

FAYE SWENGEL

Delaware River Panorama, from Federal Twist

Faye Swengel was married to Ben Badura, and they lived across the river in Lumberville, Pennsylvania. She studied at PAFA and studied under Daniel Garber. In Bucks County, she made a living carrying out portrait commissions and painting restoration work. She painted landscapes for her own work and visited Raven Rock numerous times to paint its charming views.

WILLIAM F. TAYLOR

Skating on the Canal

Taylor was born in Hamilton, Ontario, Canada, but came to the area via New York, achieving a career as a lithographer and newspaper artist. He was part of the group of artists that studied at Phillips Mill. He was also a preservationist, and in 1930, he bought and restored the Cuttalossa Inn below Lumberville. He was the first president of the Delaware Valley Protective Association, which was founded to preserve the natural

Bill Tinsman with a drawing by William Lathrop showing the Lumberville–Raven Rock Bridge before 1903. *Courtesy of Bill Tinsman.*

beauty of Bucks County. During the 1940s, artists were blamed for the deterioration of the old Lumberville–Raven Rock covered bridge. Locals claimed that if the artists had not painted it so often for its picturesque qualities, then it might have been replaced with a modern one before the old one fell apart and was closed in 1945. Barbara Coar was one of the outspoken citizens who suggested keeping the old covered bridge. William F. Taylor stated that preserving historic structures promoted higher property values. His impressionistic paintings are certainly a testament to the beauty of the area he loved.

KURT WIESE

Raven Rock Idyll, watercolor, collection of W.H. Wulfleck, Kingwood, New Jersey

Wiese was a gifted illustrator, published numerous children's books and lived on a farm in Kingwood Township, New Jersey. He was German born and worked in China in the 1930s. He taught English there, and after his release as a Japanese prisoner of war, he returned to Germany to illustrate books for children. Wiese traveled extensively in Brazil and New York, where he married; he then moved close to Raven Rock. He continued to do create numerous children's books, and he even illustrated the original *Bambi* story in 1929.

VALENTINE D'OGRIES

Four stained-glass panels: two images of saints in a traditional style and the panels *Crucifixion* and *Pattern* done in an abstract manner

D'Ogries was a friend of Geoffrey Roberts and Sorby and lived in Lambertville. He was a stained-glass artisan, restored artwork and made picture frames. D'Ogries even painted a portrait of Geoffery Roberts and was another New Yorker who moved to the area when Sorby came to Raven Rock.

Dorothy Hotchkiss

Stained-glass panels in abstract style called *Amber* and *Blue Enamel*

Unnamed Artist

Photographic portrait of George W. Robinson, storekeeper and postmaster of Raven Rock from 1889 to 1930

The work of these twenty-four artists represents most of the important artists working in the Delaware Valley in the early twentieth century. The show was a testament to the tenacity of a few local folks who really cared and did something about helping their community. Two years after the show, the road was completed. The highway improved the lives of the inhabitants, but it also took some of the charm away, with the high-speed vehicles that travel the Daniel Bray Highway. Eventually, the people who now come for the beautiful state park that is on Bull's Island replaced the artists who painted here. The beauty and charm of a backwater like Raven Rock was appealing to the artists here and to many who have come afterward. The village still attracts creative people from all walks of life who want solitude and desire to be closer to nature.

Raven Rock, the Missing Link

John Kellogg

In 1911, Governor Woodrow Wilson proposed a scenic drive along the Delaware River from Trenton to Frenchtown. It took fifty years and four governors to complete this highway from Trenton to Bull's Island and another section from the Byram Point Pleasant Bridge in Kingwood Township to Frenchtown. Still, there was a 1.9-mile stretch between Raven Rock and Byram that became known as the "Missing Link."

Initially, a concrete pavement was laid from Trenton through Lambertville to Stockton, and it was called the Delaware River Drive. In 1934, Fred H. Snipes, a Frenchtown merchant and a director of the Delaware River Drive Association, petitioned Governor Harold Hoffman to complete the roadway. In 1935, Governor Hoffman ordered the construction of a three-mile section of the highway from Frenchtown south. Construction on the phase was halted for a few years during the depression and World War II. Later, Senator Samuel L. Bodine of Flemington, a longtime advocate of the Delaware River Drive, and Assemblyman Emmert Wilson of Stockton urged Governor Alfred E. Driscoll to construct another three-mile section. In 1949, the roadway was extended north from Stockton to Raven Rock. It took another five years for the northern section of the road to be completed south to Byram.

In 1959, Senator Wesley Lance and Assemblyman Raymond Bowkley pushed for the completion of the highway. The construction of this last

The old roadway was obviously inadequate for modern vehicles, as seen in this newspaper photograph from the 1950s. *Courtesy of the* Hunterdon Democrat.

section proved to be the most difficult. The new roadway was adjacent to a small mountain in Byram. More than sixty thousand cubic yards of rock had to be blasted away without damaging nearby railroad tracks and homes. Franklin Contracting Company of Little Falls, New Jersey, was awarded the job for $542,388. Construction was completed near the end of October 1959.

The new roadway was open to traffic for the first time in late November. A flaw in the newly laid pavement forced the closure of the new roadway after a week. Experimental gravel placed during the first course of paving caused soft spots to appear on the surface. Traffic was forced to detour to the old dirt road until repairs were completed the following June.

This factual account of the evolution of the road does not convey the frustrations faced by the residents of Raven Rock as they sought to have the Missing Link completed. Although the State of New Jersey constructed the Delaware River Drive both south (1949) and north (1954) of Raven Rock, it disclaimed responsibility for linking the two segments together. Barbara Coar was a Raven Rock resident who led the long fight to get the strip of dirt road paved so that residents could get relief from the clouds of heavy dust stirred up by heavy traffic. In a letter to Governor Robert Meyner, she wrote:

> *I have asked Commissioner Palmer (of the State Highway Department) to study the material you furnished me. The Commissioner reports that the portion of the road which concerns your group is a municipal road and not a State highway. He further states that as a matter of highway planning he sees no occasion for the State to acquire the strip. Apparently, the State supplied some calcium chloride last year because of some surface disturbance, which had been caused in connection with adjacent construction. It is the feeling of the Highway Department that the matter is a local one which should be discussed with municipal officials.*

He recommended that the residents approach Delaware and Kingwood Township officials to assess their interest in funding this project. Understandably, the municipal officials had no intention of funding what was obviously a state project. It wasn't until 1959 that Governor Robert Meyner, at the urging of Senator Wesley Lance and Assemblyman Raymond Bowldy, committed the state to the construction of the Missing Link.

With the Delaware River Drive complete from Trenton to Frenchtown in 1954, except for the Missing Link, Raven Rock residents were subjected to more traffic through the village than they had ever experienced. It was particularly bad on weekends, when swarms of sightseeing motorists were out for a drive along the river. Driving either north from Stockton or south from Frenchtown on the new roadway, they suddenly came to an old dusty dirt road in Raven Rock. Mrs. Hannah Updegrove, speaking for Raven Rock housewives, told the Delaware Township Committee in 1958 that for the past five years, life in Raven Rock was almost "unbearable" due to the great increase in traffic over the narrow road through the built-up section of Raven Rock. She reported that dust from cars makes it impossible to open windows in the heat of summer and that her front porch is less than three feet from the road, causing flying rocks and splashing water to hit against her windows.

When local residents complained to the state about the condition of their roadway, the state's response was to give them calcium chloride to keep the dust down instead of providing them with a new highway. Here, residents are spreading calcium chloride for a photo in the local paper. In the background are the Williamson and Johnson-Feeney Houses. *Courtesy of the* Hunterdon Democrat.

In 1956, Raven Rock residents were forced to make their own road repairs, if only symbolically. For more than two years, they tried to get the State Highway Department to at least oil the road to cut down on the dust caused by heavy traffic and to fill in potholes, which were rampant. Led by Barbara Coar, their pleas went unheeded by the state. Although Commissioner Palmer promised in 1954 to provide Delaware Township with sufficient calcium chloride to halt the dust conditions, none ever materialized. What particularly incensed the residents of Raven Rock was the fact that the State Highway Department allotted $8,000 to Delaware Township to improve Federal Twist Road on which only nine homes were situated, but it couldn't spare the money to spread calcium chloride on the more heavily traveled road through Raven Rock. A picture appeared in the *Trenton Sunday Times* on August 19, 1956, showing eight women from Raven Rock spreading the one bag of calcium chloride that they had on the road. This symbolic protest was hardly sufficient to deal with the dust on 1.9 miles of dirt road.

There were two citizen groups that became strong advocates for the completion of the Delaware River Drive. The Delaware Valley Protective Association was founded in 1933. This influential organization had a large membership in New Jersey and Pennsylvania dedicated to preserving the beauty of the Delaware Valley. The Citizen's Committee for the Completion of Route 29 was a spontaneous movement that was originated at a meeting called in early 1958 by the Frenchtown Civic Association to focus attention on the need for the immediate completion of the Missing Link.

In August 1949, financing was secured for the construction of a three-mile section of roadway from Stockton to Raven Rock. Senator Samuel Bodine announced an appropriation of $360,000. The actual cost after the project was put out for bid was $272,000. The project called for fifty thousand cubic yards of earth excavation and twenty thousand cubic yards of rock excavation. When the State Highway Department announced that a right-of-way of 150 feet would be needed for this project, residents expressed their fear that homes adjacent to the new road would be damaged. The chief highway engineer for the state sought to allay these fears by promising that no properties would be damaged by the arbitrary insistence of a 150-foot right-of-way. Unfortunately, the C.F. Lowman house, which was located within the 150-foot right-of-way, was acquired by the state and demolished. This new section of the Delaware River Drive, which is 24 feet wide, with an 8-foot shoulder, opened without any ceremony in September 1950.

In November 1952, Senator Bodine announced to the surprise of many that the completion of the Missing Link through Raven Rock had been assured beyond a reasonable doubt. He reported that Governor Driscoll would approve $1 million from the current year's budget and $2 million from next year's budget for the construction of the entire distance from Raven Rock to Kingwood Station. Two alternate routes would be studied to determine if the new road would be built immediately adjacent to the Bel-Del Division of the Pennsylvania Railroad or if a road more remote from the railroad would be desirable. It was ultimately decided to align the road adjacent to the railroad.

In June 1953, contracts were awarded for the construction of a three-mile segment south from Kingwood Station toward Byram. This section was deemed to be the most challenging since much blasting was required to cut a path for the highway through the hills adjacent to the railroad. In January 1954, the State Highway Department advertised for bids for the grading of the last section through Raven Rock to the southern terminus of the section then under construction one mile north of Byram. Unfortunately, both Republican governor Driscoll and Senator Bodine left office in January 1954. The new governor, Democrat Robert Meyner, did not support this project, stating, "I don't believe in building roads that go nowhere."

Frustrated residents of Raven Rock met with Delaware Township officials at the home of Barbara Coar in August 1956 to plan a strategy for getting the state to act on completing the Missing Link. Several residents called the dirt road stretch a political football. It was started as a Republican project, but since the Democrats had come to power in Trenton, nothing was to be done. Miss Coar read a letter from State Highway commissioner Dwight Palmer, which she interpreted as implying she was a crank. Delaware Township committeeman Frank Curtis reported to the group that when the paved portion is completed, it would be along a new right-of-way closer to the river that will eliminate the half-mile stretch of curved road that at that time was directly adjacent to the village's homes.

The Meyner administration claimed that he road didn't belong to the state, despite the fact that they had constructed the sections north and south of the village. Barbara Coar was determined to prove otherwise. Searching through Kingwood Township records, she came across a letter dated August 23, 1954, written by A. Lee Grover, commissioner of the State Highway Department. Addressed to the Kingwood Township Clerk, the letter stated, "I am directed to forward to you the enclosed certified copy of a Determination Order made by State Highway Commissioner Dwight R.G. Palmer under date of August 20, 1954, taking over as part of the State Highway system for construction and maintenance after construction that portion of legislated Route 29A [1927] Route 29 [1953] as shown on red on the attached plan." The legal description of the portion shown in red clearly documented that the state had responsibility for the road through Raven Rock.

It appears that documentation of state responsibility led Commissioner Palmer to announce in early 1957 that the Missing Link

The Missing Link indicated on a map, with a photo of a car in a ditch on the road through Raven Rock. *Courtesy of the* Hunterdon Democrat.

would be completed if funds were made available in the next state budget on July 1. Senator Wesley Lance applauded this announcement, stating that the Missing Link was a "much needed improvement in order to utilize to full advantage money that has already been spent by the State for building a road between Stockton and Frenchtown." Raven Rock residents' hopes were crushed when Governor Meyner proposed a budget for the next fiscal year that did not include funds for the completion of the Missing Link.

Residents of the Delaware Valley were determined that the 1.9-mile Missing Link needed to be completed immediately. To demonstrate broad-based support for their cause, the Frenchtown Civic Association, the Delaware Valley Protective Association and the Citizens Committee for the Completion of Route 29 conducted a Missing Link petition campaign. The campaign was successfully completed on February 17, 1958, with more than 2,600 signatures. A request was made to Senator Lance that he arrange for the leaders of the campaign to present the petition to Governor Meyner.

Leaders of the petition campaign had a cool reception when they met with Governor Meyner on March 24, 1958. He told the group that the state had no appropriation for highway projects that do not qualify for federal aid. He said that the legislature would have to pass a one-cent increase in the state's gasoline tax for such projects. The governor gave little hope for the project even if the gasoline tax increase were approved. "We are going to evaluate road needs in terms of which serves the greatest good, not in terms of who makes the greatest noise," Meyner stated.

In May 1958, the Missing Link Art Show was held in Barbara Coar's house (Raven Rock's old post office) to call attention to the deplorable condition of the dirt road that runs through the village. Organized by B.A. Sorby, secretary of the Citizens Committee for the Completion of Route 29, the exhibit featured some excellent paintings of some of the nation's best artists who had either painted scenes along the Missing Link or had made their home in the vicinity. Proceeds from the show went to a fund to further the campaign to focus attention on the imperative need for immediate completion of the road project that had been abandoned by the State Highway Department since 1954.

It was with great relief when Raven Rock residents learned that their dream to see the Missing Link completed was about to be realized. Speaking at a memorial service in April 1959 for the late Senator Samuel Bodine, one of the staunchest supporters of the Delaware River Drive, Governor Robert Meyner announced that the Missing Link would be completed by the end of the year. He explained his change in support for funding this project on the availability of funds from the one-cent increase in the state gasoline tax approved in 1958. It is likely that Senator Wesley Lance was instrumental in the governor's change of position on this project. In 1959, Senator Lance became president of the New Jersey Senate. As the Republican head of one of the houses of the state legislature in a Democratic administration, his longtime support of the completion of the Missing Link certainly led him to negotiate a deal with the Governor's Office for an appropriation for this project.

Work began in late June. The alignment was set between the railroad and the twelve- to sixteen-foot dirt road that it would replace. The new alignment did not require the costly realignment of a portion of the railroad that had previously been considered, and it eliminated two existing railroad crossings for through traffic on the new highway. The new road was designed for two twenty-five-foot lanes with ten-foot shoulders. More than sixty thousand cubic tons of earth and rock were required to be moved. Nearly fifty-five thousand cubic yards came from cutting down a high hill in Byram and were used as fill in Raven Rock. Between sixteen and twenty tons of dynamite were required to break up the tough trap rock. Lloyds of London was the only firm that the contractor could get to insure the job from damages resulting from the blasting.

One problem encountered early on in the construction was the soggy bed of an old gristmill pond that proved to be an obstacle in building a firm substrate for the new roadway. The old millpond, locally referred to as the "slough," kept filling with water from underground sources. More than 4,500 cubic yards of muck and wet sand were removed and replaced with an equal amount of dry sand and gravel fill, yet wet spots reappeared. Pumping was resorted to, and finally a stable base was achieved. The pond was also used for water for the railroad engines that used to stop at Raven Rock Station.

One victim of the construction of the missing link was the destruction of the home of Mr. and Mrs. George Emmons, who had lived in their home for forty-three years. B.A. Sorby wrote that Raven Rock residents expressed regret and bewilderment with the State Highway Department's action in view of their repeated statements that none of the homes in Raven Rock would be taken. These emotions were intensified with the realization that the Emmons homesite was not needed for the highway construction. The shoulder of the new highway was twenty-two feet more distant from the front of their home than the old dirt road.

August 12, 1960, was a great day of celebration in Raven Rock. An estimated three hundred people gathered in the village to pay tribute to Captain Daniel Bray and to formally dedicate the Daniel Bray Highway. Legislation sponsored by Senator Wesley Lance renamed the Delaware River Drive in honor of the Revolutionary War hero from Hunterdon County who collected the boats for George Washington's historic crossing of the Delaware River.

The Missing Link had just been completed. About twenty-five direct descendants of Daniel Bray were present to hear both Governor Robert Meyner and State Highway commissioner Dwight Palmer praise the Revolutionary War hero and dedicate the new highway in his memory.

Heath-Updegrove House on the Missing Link, circa 1940s. *Courtesy of Luverne Updegrove Caulton.*

In his remarks, Governor Meyner noted that this peaceful valley had been spared much of the transformation wrought by twentieth-century industrialization and that if he were to return to the valley today, Captain Bray would still find familiar scenes.

Commissioner Palmer's remarks were cut short by a 107-car freight train that passed through Raven Rock while he was speaking. The ceremonies were held outdoors, with the speaker's platform set up near the historic old sycamore tree in Raven Rock. This is the same tree in Daniel Garber's painting *Our Country Neighbors*. Senator Lance served as master of ceremonies. Following the ceremony, the Delaware Valley Protective Association held an open house at the old Raven Rock Post Office, where dioramas of the Battle of Trenton and a replica of a Durham boat, the type Captain Bray collected for Washington, were on display.

QUARRYING IN RAVEN ROCK

Bill Saja

Aptly named Raven Rock, the pure physical dominance of rock overwhelmingly commands the landscape. Ancient homes nestled at its base seemingly play a timeless game of danger with this imposing adversary. The cliffs are sedentary, napping, taking rest from past labors. While the rock tangibly dominates the hamlet, the force it had is becoming a distant memory. Raven Rock brownstone built countless structures throughout New Jersey, New York and Pennsylvania. Nature has reclaimed the quarry. Navigation through forest overgrowth is needed to explore it today. Sections of the thick cables still cross the quarry floor. Parts of equipment, frames and sheds mix with overgrowth. The quarry pond has filled with fallen trees of past decades. But the cuts of quarrymen into the rock face are still clear. It's a place of history and transition, of toil and pleasure. The abandoned artifacts relate the labors of a century past. Still, for those seasoned locals, mention of the quarry brings a distant gleam to their eye, and a smile illuminates their faces as they relive youthful memories of summer fun and excitement at the best swimming hole around, along with notions of what was at the bottom of the pond.

Unidentified house atop the quarry on Quarry Road. Note the steam plants used to power the tools in the quarry and the derricks used to move stone. *Courtesy of Luverne Updegrove Caulton.*

Raven Rock

The geologic information on Raven Rock indicates that it was formed in the late Triassic period, approximately 185 to 155 million years ago, the age of Pangaea experiencing demise and the Atlantic Ocean being birthed. Within this time, a great fault created several block mountains with wide, low basins. Sand-laden rivers carried sediments into the basins from the uplifted mountains that eroded away through the ages. Natural cementation of these sediments transformed the product into sandstone deposits known as the Newark Group.

Several different types or formations exist within the Newark Group. These relate to the mineral composition and formation process of the stone. Climate, deposition and erosion commonly create fingers of intrusion between formations. Argillite is dense, well-cemented sandstone of varying dark colors known as the Lockatong Formation. Arkose is sandstone in which at least a quarter of its grains are feldspar. It is commonly reddish in color and is the stone of the Stockton

Formation. Raven Rock is composed of arkose with the occasional overlay of argillite. It is the arkose that gave rise to the brownstone quarry industry.

BROWNSTONE

Brownstone quarries were different animals in comparison to trap rock quarries of today. It was a selective process of quarrying for specific purposes. Cutting, shaping and seasoning the stone were additional steps. It was an industry of craftsmanship as well as production.

Brownstone was the most popular building stone between the late eighteenth century and early twentieth century. Stockton stone was recognized as the finest in the Delaware Valley. Stockton brownstone, quarried at Prallsville, was used to build Nassau Hall at Princeton University. Stockton brownstone was used to build countless homes, churches, libraries, train stations, schools, bridges and public buildings. Brownstone gained popularity as part of the Romantic movement that took hold in the 1840s. This movement urged the use of natural colors like green or brown in contrast to the white of Greek Revival architecture. Brownstone was suited to the predominant Italianate architecture seen in villas of the wealthy and row houses of the middle class, including the famous New York brownstone fronts. Brownstone conveyed substance, permanence and status and was chosen for landmark structures. Of the thirty thousand buildings in New York City in 1880, 78.6 percent were constructed of brownstone.

ANCIENT QUARRYING

Members of the Fox Creek culture (two thousand to one thousand years ago) are thought to have quarried argillite in the Raven Rock area. Argillite blanks and tools were used for trading. Artifacts having origins in the hills of this locale have been found within excavations of villages in Monmouth County. Argillite tools and weapons were probably utilized as early as the Archaic period (ten thousand to eight thousand years ago), but artifacts have yet to be found. Weathering affects argillite rapidly, thus artifacts are rare. The first Europeans supplanted the wooden or fieldstone grave markers with sandstone. The ability to make inscriptions allowed a more permanent memorial; however, the properties that allowed these carvings also allowed deterioration and weathering.

ECONOMICS AND QUARRIES

Economic turbulence was common in later nineteenth-century America. It was a cyclical boom/bust experience, with monopolies well entrenched and corruption rampant at all levels of government. The Civil War from 1860 to 1865 tore the nation apart, and the Reconstruction era was ended by mandate in 1877. The Panic of 1873 left 3 million people unemployed and collapsed farm prices, creating great rural poverty. Recovery began five years later in 1878. Only the Great Depression of the 1930s exceeded the Panic of 1893. One in six Americans was jobless. By the end of 1893, there were more than 16,000 business failures, including 156 railroads and more than 500 banks. This depression lasted four years, with recovery beginning in 1897.

Everyone felt the effects of the national panics locally. Quarries witnessed cancelled orders and little prospect for short-term recovery. Many simply suspended operations, while heavily financed ventures failed. Workers had no safety nets or benefits and faced years of uncertainty trying to survive.

DELAWARE TOWNSHIP QUARRIES

Brownstone quarrying began in earnest after the completion of the feeder canal in the 1830s. Transportation for stone was now feasible. Between the 1830s and 1850s, the major share of quarrying was performed in Prallsville and Stockton, but most work was limited to stone that could be used locally on the canal and bridges and in construction of the railroad. Still, stone was selected for the construction of churches and buildings in Trenton, Camden and Philadelphia. Construction of the Belvidere & Delaware Railroad in the 1850s was the vehicle to launch brownstone as a major industry within Delaware Township.

John Prall opened the quarries in Prallsville in 1830 or 1831. Stonecutters used this stone to build the railroad bridge across the Delaware between Lambertville and New Hope. Behind the Stockton House, a quarry was opened in 1832 by Asher Johnson. It was a supplier of stone for bridge building on the Lehigh Valley Railroad. Asher Wolverton also owned a quarry along the feeder canal. However, the Panic of 1873 closed these for years.

The Raven Rock Quarry was a source of stone for the construction of the feeder canal and the Belvidere & Delaware Railroad. The first mention of the Raven Rock Quarry, as a business entity, noted that it was opened in 1873–74 by Nolan Brothers. Dennis McAvoy was the foreman, and John Steel was the first workman. The duration and scope of Nolan Brothers' venture is lost to time. Strong indications are that quarry operations were transferred to the Delaware & Raritan Canal Company before 1880. In this year, the company employed fifteen men in Raven Rock, while the other quarries stood silent.

View of Raven Rock Quarry with a spur line from the Bel-Del rail line in the foreground. Note the chicken coops on the Rodman-Laszlo farmstead on the hill. *Courtesy of Luverne Updegrove Caulton.*

Recovery in the early 1880s again started the boom cycle in Delaware Township's brownstone industry. By summer of 1882, all the quarries in the township were planned to be operational. In 1884, the quarry at Raven Rock was again under new supervision. Hutchinson & Brothers and Bull's Island Stone Quarries advertised all kinds of stone cut to order. Belgian blocks, curbing, sills, lintels, steps and capping were constantly on hand, in large quantity. Building and dimension stone was available and shipped by railroad or water.

By 1899, the Stockton Stone Company quarried at Raven Rock. John Ledger was manager, with George Sutton, Oscar Sargent and M.F. Berger as quarrymen. The date of company incorporation, January 12, 1897, was just as recovery was beginning from the Panic of 1893. Its principal place of business, 26 Exchange Place Jersey City, was the transportation and financial center erected by the Pennsylvania Railroad, the controlling entity of the former Belvidere & Delaware Railroad and the Delaware & Raritan Canal Company. In the early 1890s, special stone trains transported excellent building blocks from the quarries to construct the heavy Norman Gothic–styled stations at Somerville, Raritan, North Branch and Bayonne.

The twentieth century marked change in architectural design and taste, returning to a Neoclassical focus for landmark buildings. It was a time when the suburbs began, and the skyscraper moved from infancy to adolescence. The material of the new age was cheaper, more versatile and much more suited to fit the needs of a modern society. Concrete supplanted brownstone as the material of choice.

Life of the Quarry

Brownstone quarrying was a seasonal industry. Usually, it began in April and ended in November. Brownstone is laden with water, and freezing weather simply resulted in damaged stone. The production year was limited, between the last frost and the first frost, but the work was intense, six days a week and most days from sunrise to sundown. Labor was taken from a core of a few steady employees and a mixture of transient new labor. The core labor enjoyed the benefit of working winter months, doing maintenance on equipment, clearing debris and readying for the upcoming season.

The initial steps in opening a quarry are to strip away all trees and vegetation from the surface above the sandstone deposit. After the deforestation, soil and all other stone are removed to gain access to the layered sandstone. Trees cut during the clearing could be used for construction or as fuel. Upon exposing the brownstone deposit, inspection of the layering of the stone would be done by a geologist, rock boss or prospector to determine where to cut the stone. The most efficient method was to quarry where the stone was regularly layered and cut by angular or irregular fractures.

Quarry work in the nineteenth century was a labor-intensive industry, a process of muscle rather than mechanization. It utilized a channel and wedging process where channels were cut into the stone on three sides of the rock face, and wedges were then placed into the channels to split off the stone block. Workers used drills, pickaxes, sledgehammers and wedges to crack the block away from the layer. The block was then taken to the scrabbling area for cutting and seasoning.

Workmen drilled a series of one-inch holes along a line. Small half-round iron bars called feathers were inserted in these holes, with a small steel wedge inserted between the feathers and rock. Workmen would strike the feathers with sledgehammers until stress split the stone, producing a rough-shaped slab. Cutting of the stone was the final step in the process. This was performed by a series of steel blades moved along the desired cutting plane while the stone was secured to the cutting surface. Multiple cuts were utilized, while the blades were cooled by water with abrasives added to the stream.

The use of black powder was not preferred due to stone loss, and it was used only as a last resort, on dense stone. Methods such as the "Knox patented system of blasting" and the Lewising system allowed some successful quarrying with powder with limited stone loss. Dynamite was almost never used in the quarrying process but was feasible with rubble. Blasting was used in clearing the quarry floor of debris stone and creating cellar stone.

Movement of the brownstone blocks about the quarry was performed by slings, wagons and sleds powered by mules, horses or oxen. Late in the brownstone age, narrow-gauge railways became popular. Derricks were also utilized, set perpendicular to the quarry floor, with cable capabilities allowing mechanized stone movement. Steam drills and technological

Small metal shed that was used to store explosives for quarrying, if needed. The apparatus in the trees is the remains of the derrick that was used to move large stones. *Photo by R. Curt Chinnici.*

improvements in the channeling process improved production. All this equipment and activity were utilized in Raven Rock over the decades from the 1870s through the 1930s.

Brownstone is porous. Moisture accounts for the stone's ability to be easily shaped; however, it also makes the stone susceptible to cracking and flaking. Once quarried, blocks were removed to the scrabbling area for cutting and seasoning. The water in the stone was called "sap." Seasoning or drying the stone to remove "sap" was an aging process of several months in which the stone was covered with soil. After about four months, the stone should have achieved the proper seasoning. The surfaces were considered case-hardened and resistant to weathering. Since frost could destroy unseasoned stone, ingenious protective methods were used in winter months. The Hummelstown quarry placed the unseasoned stone in pits and covered the stone with heavy coats of manure to ward off the cold.

Quarrymen

Life as a quarryman was a profession to which few of us would select to aspire. The physical nature of the work was suited only for the young and fit. Child labor was very common and, in many instances, a necessity for family survival. Records of the Hummelstown quarry indicate that 25 percent of the company's workforces within the 1880s were made up of children. Mining, quarrying, agriculture and any endeavor requiring manual labor employed children as cheap help. During this time, more than 50 percent of a worker's wages were spent solely for food. Children were expected to work to help feed the family.

During the last quarter of the nineteenth century, a vast majority of quarry workers were immigrants from Italy. This fact is confirmed by the U.S. censuses for 1870, 1880 and 1900. Italians had lots of experience working stone quarries in their homeland and may have been some of the itinerant quarrymen who worked here.

Shelter for transient labor was simple, likely in the form of sheds in or around the quarry. Simple wooden structures with perhaps a stove and little more than a bed, but no plumbing or running water, kept one removed from the elements. Shelter fit the minimum needs of the period. The environment offered fresh water and waste disposal. Work was daily and intense, so nothing was needed beyond this spartan existence. By the late 1930s, these sheds had long disappeared, and nothing remains today of these tiny homes or shelters in Raven Rock.

By middle age, quarrymen who had paid their dues through labor progressions should have mercifully moved to a strenuous but manageable supervisory or artisan role. The dangers of the quarry were vast, and over time, everyone's luck eventually runs out. Accidents were frequent, and bruised and smashed fingers, hands, toes and feet were common. Loss of appendages and limbs was an occupational hazard. Occasionally, fatalities occurred from falling slabs; collapsing walls; cable, derrick and machinery accidents; and other mishaps.

A terrible explosion occurred at B&EW Twinning's Quarry in Prallsville on May 19, 1888. The cause of the explosion remains uncertain, but the story relates that James Wafer, forty years old and the quarry boss, went to the powder magazine at about 7:30 a.m. A few moments later, the magazine was blown to pieces by a thunderous blast, and unfortunately, Mr. Wafer had the same fate. Workers were thrown about from the concussion but survived their injuries. It is believed that the magazine housed 300 to 350 small kegs of black powder and about fifty cans of dynamite. A deep crater was all that remained of the powder house. More than a dozen buildings were destroyed within a quarter mile radius of the magazine. Homes in Prallsville were damaged, and windows were blown out a mile away. It was said that the blast could be heard in Trenton and New Brunswick.

For days afterward, curiosity seekers numbering in the thousands flocked to the site to view the carnage and devastation. Mr. Wafer was career quarryman with twenty years' experience working with explosives. He was to be married the following Thursday. The wedding ring intended for his fiancée needed resizing, and Mr. Wafer picked it up several days earlier and wore it on one of his own fingers. Late on the day of the blast, the ring was discovered on a Stockton Street, three quarters of a mile from the blast.

END OF BROWNSTONE AND PEAK OF IMPRESSIONISTS

The Raven Rock Quarry closed for commercial brownstone quarrying in the 1930s. As the brownstone era ended, Pennsylvania impressionist painters were in their heyday. Characterized by landscapes and color, the New Hope group of artists found the areas of the Delaware around Raven Rock irresistible. They strove to capture the moment with their oil paintings. Striations of stone and varying hues of color against the natural background of the seasons were the inspiration for beautiful landscapes. Daniel Garber, Edward Redfield, Ben Badura and Fern Coppedge were among the artist who captured the area and the rock within their works.

WE'RE GONNA BE RICH

"Norton, my ship is coming in, and it's the *Queen Mary.*" Jackie Gleason seemed to utter phrases like this to Art Carney in every episode of *The Honeymooners*, time after time believing that he had found his treasure. In the mid-1950s, Vernon and Alvin Gatling brought the Raven Rock Quarry back to life. They created their own bittersweet comedy, believing that their ship was about to arrive, but just like Gleason, they waited for the boat at the airport.

The uranium craze hit America in the early 1950s. The atomic age brought the promise of unlimited energy from nuclear plants throughout the country. The fuel for these plants would be refined from uranium ore. A frenzy of prospecting for the ore, akin to the California gold rush, swept the nation. Geiger counters were a must, with amateur prospectors spending every free minute at obscure sites, hoping that the instrument would screech that they were rich. Every newspaper and magazines such as *Life* did cover stories on radioactive fever and uranium strikes. An episode of *The Lucy & Desi Comedy Hour* was devoted to the craze, as the pair spent their weekend camping with Fred and Ethel Mertz in comical pursuit of the elusive element.

Vernon and Alvin Gatling lived in South River, New Jersey. Vernon, twenty-eight, graduated college in Ohio and spent a year at Rutgers Law School in Newark before taking a position as a law clerk at a New York Law firm. Alvin, twenty-five, dropped out of college after his sophomore year. Both were bitten by the uranium bug and spent hours in the New York Public Library studying the subject and convincing themselves that they would hit it big. Their adventures made all of Ralph Kramden's schemes and dilemmas look like a mere bag of shells. The Gatlings prospected in Utah and Colorado, allegedly purchasing 40 acres of uranium-rich land in Utah. They claimed to have forty-eight options of claim on 960 acres of land in Colorado, too. When prospects did not pan out, they decided to head back east to find locations to score their jackpot.

Upon their return to New Jersey, they searched areas of promise in Hunterdon and Mercer Counties. One day, they happened to appear at Shuck's garage in Stockton. Anton Schuck gave permission to use their Geiger counters in the quarry now owned by Schuck. He believed that

The Gattling brothers, Vernon and Alvin, who "discovered" uranium in the Raven Rock Quarry in the 1950s. *Courtesy of the* Hunterdon Democrat.

they were college students from Rutgers doing studies or just out for some adventure. A few months passed, and the Gatlings made another visit to ask if they could perform some test borings. Anton agreed, and a few days later, some borings were left at his garage, with the Gatling's opinion that the results were not promising.

Schuck forgot about the Gatling brothers until some weeks later, when a friend asked about the people working Anton's quarry. Anton was unaware of any activity other than allowing the Gatlings access months earlier. He discovered the Gatlings and a crew of workmen from Pevar Construction. There was drilling equipment and a primitive wooden walkway across the pond to the quarry wall. A shaft for the access tunnel was started into the face of the quarry wall. Anton ordered everyone off the property and thought the matter was over.

What Anton Schuck did not know was that the Gatlings believed they had found mineable uranium. They formed a corporation, Gatling Brothers Mining and Development, and prepared a lease for the property that was notarized and filed in Hunterdon County. The county clerk advised the Gatlings that the unsigned lease was not valid, but the brothers believed that the filing would give them standing. Shortly, the Gatlings resumed operations. Schuck, along with his attorney, C. Lloyd Fisher, and Sheriff William Amerman, visited the quarry to again eject the Gatlings. They discovered one worker from Pevar operating an air drill who willingly left. Pevar Construction was hired to drill the initial access tunnel and became a stockholder of the Gatlings' company, purchasing their shares through services rendered.

Newspapers headlined the fantastic uranium strike in Raven Rock. It was featured on radio and local television news from Philadelphia to New York. Scores of amateur prospectors and hundreds of curiosity seekers made a pilgrimage to the quarry as the legal process dragged on. The story grew as geological experts gave interviews and opinions. Speculation of the ore's worth became astronomical. Delaware Township claimed that it should have a share of proceeds since it was being mined under a public road. Everyone was counting their millions, while Anton Schuck was paying his attorney, fighting a fraudulent lease and trying to simply make a living in the middle of a media circus.

The Gatlings' motives in creating the uranium find of the century are unknown. They may have become addicted to their dream of wealth and began to believe their own fantasy. Alvin was a patient at the Marlboro Psychiatric Hospital in 1954. Records indicate that he had been committed there for about six weeks. Incorporation filings for the Gatling's company occurred only three weeks after Alvin's release. Vernon's dream, coupled with his marginal legal expertise, set him on a path of spending his dream fortune before the first day of prospecting began. In the eighteen months between the birth of Gatling Mining and Development, and the evictions from the quarry, the brothers established headquarters in a fashionable New Brunswick office building, furnished it with new décor and purchased new executive wardrobes and a new Cadillac. Vernon could sell his dream, offering stock for services to Pevar Construction and several attorneys who would be company counsels, as well as selling shares to family and friends and others at twenty-five cents per share.

Within the same period, the Gatlings were locked out and evicted from their corporate offices for nonpayment and bouncing their first rent check and sued by Morris Cohen, owner of New Jersey Typewriter Service, to retrieve the office furnishings bought on unpaid credit and held by the Gatlings' landlord. They had judgments entered against them by Wallach's of New York for nonpayment of clothing purchases and had the Cadillac repossessed for nonpayment. Besides, the brothers had gone through three different attorneys and had been summoned twice by the Securities and Exchange Commission (SEC) due to irregularities

Quarry wall with large hole from where the men dug an access opening to mine uranium from Anton Schuck's quarry. *Courtesy of the* Hunterdon Democrat.

and possibly violating laws pertaining to their sale of public stock. The Gatlings had multiple judgments issued against them and had already been charged and released on bond for bouncing checks. They faced new charges, including investigation by a Middlesex County Grand Jury for issuing worthless checks.

After months of legal wrangling, nature continually filling the quarry ponds and growing anger from people coming to the realization that this dream was simply a nightmare, the Gatlings' options became limited. The SEC had the brothers in its crosshairs. Their attorneys explained that the brothers ignored their advice, and each attorney ultimately dropped them as clients. Their credit was worthless. Vernon could no longer sell his dream to anyone, and Gatling Mining and Development pulled out of Raven Rock. In a final desperate move, the Gatlings brought a damage suit against Anton Schuck for $57.8 million, seeking mineral rights for mining the property. After additional legal proceedings, agreement was made that the Gatlings should produce an expert to confirm the claims that a profitable venture could be established at the quarry. Expert confirmation would allow the venture to move forward. No such expert was produced, and the suit was dismissed.

With the dismissal, the story faded away. But unlike the schemes of Ralph Kramden, who simply hurt himself, the Gatlings brought misfortune to many. They became addicted to their dream and used others to finance their fantasy. Unlike Gleason's character, there were no moments of redemption, making amends, reconciliation or the seeking of forgiveness. The Gatlings simply faded as a distant memory, but their story of deception is still fresh half a century later.

The quarry became quiet again except for teenagers looking for a swim on a hot summer day. Betty Schuck Davis, daughter of Anton Schuck, related that her father put some old bicycles in the pond to discourage diving. Slowly, nature again took back the quarry. Trees grew and plants covered old paths. The pond became clogged with fallen trees. The swimming hole became a memory. Just a few feet off Quarry Road and only a stone's throw from Route 29, this part of the rock is hidden and quiet, and it seems to be at rest again.

Remarkable Raven Rock Residents

Carolyn M. Nicklen

Persons of interest have been making their mark on this appealing land, at the confluence of the Delaware River and Bull's Creek, long before the seventeenth-century Europeans gave this place, or these life-giving waters, their current names.

We are fortunate to have some record of the ordinary and often extraordinary stories of these people. These records were sometimes official accounts, as were the Belvidere & Delaware Railroad daily reports. Sometimes they were born of a devotion to saving local history, as were the scrapbook collections of Bertha Schuck, which are now in the public domain through the foresight of her daughter, Betty Davis. And sometimes the stories are told through the very personal reporting of a faithful diarist like Luverne Updegrove Caulton, who spent thirty years in Raven Rock.

Public Record

Let us begin in 1860 with a Bel-Del accounting of prizefighting on Bull's Island. During the first week of December, two matches were held. The pugilist Clarke defeated Harrigan after a three-hour, forty-minute contest. In the second match, two pugilists fought fifty-six rounds before the decision was awarded to Woods after King was accused of "falling without being struck at." New Jersey continued to allow pugilism after Pennsylvania declared it a crime, with the penalty of $1,000 and up to two years of solitary imprisonment.

In 1870, there was a curious Bel-Del entry about the disappearance of Mr. Hoffman, who was the Bull's Island ticket agent. It seems that he left for Philadelphia, where he declared he would never return to his Bull's Island job. We can only assume that Bull's Island was not so bad after all since he had returned within the week. Forty years later, in 1910, another (or much older) Conductor Hoffman became part of the classic early short movie "A Western Romance," which was being filmed in Raven Rock and at the Bull's Island Station, favorite shooting locations of the Edison Film Corporation.

On record in the Bel-Del chronicles were repeated references to disasters such as fires, floods, derailments and deaths that affected the residents of Raven Rock. One such disaster was the fire in 1876 that consumed the store of Lorenzo Kerr, a dwelling and a post office at Bull's Island Station. The name changed to Raven Rock Station in 1890.

One of the five most catastrophic events, the Sunset Cow Wreck of 1853, happened just as the sun was setting at Bull's Island. A gravel train, carrying 250 Irish laborers on ten very light platform cars, hit a cow that had suddenly jumped onto the tracks. As a result of the derailment, twelve workers died and twenty others were injured.

Tragically, William La Fever of Lambertville was lost on the river during the Great Flood of 1903. A house in the swirling waters hit him as he attempted to transport his friend Shird Brink, from Lumberville, Pennsylvania, to his operator's job at Raven Rock Station, New Jersey.

On February 11, 1909, it is written in the Bel-Del chronicle that "[p] eople of Raven Rock were alarmed, of late, by the strange large tracks found in the snow that were said to have been made by the 'Jersey Devil.'"

Although a towering local American sycamore, which was 150 feet high and 13 feet in circumference, does not qualify as a person of interest, it certainly had many people interested in its fate in July 1959. Its saving was chronicled in the Bel-Del records. It was to have been cut down to make room for the construction of the Daniel Bray Highway that was projected through this fair village. In the end, the tree was spared after much provocation by locals, led by Barbara Coar. The tree, long a favorite to people in the community, was the subject of the popular painting *Our Country Neighbors* by Daniel Garber. The stump of this majestic tree still exists under a shroud of vines—perhaps a candidate for a future cause.

PERSONAL RECOLLECTIONS: ANTON SCHUCK (1900–1968)

Born in Germany in 1900 and brought to Raven Rock by his Uncle Sebastian and Aunt Agnes when he was two, Anton Schuck, known locally as "Tony," was a key player in the shaping of both this village and Stockton until his death. It is to his wife, Bertha, that we owe thanks for her collections of local history.

Although they returned to Germany for a few years, by the time Tony was thirteen, he was back to stay. Sebastian and Agnes owned and worked the poultry farm just up Quarry Road. They raised chickens and sold eggs. They did this until they no longer could climb the hill to the chicken coops that were on the meadow over Raven Rock. In November 1941, they sold one thousand chickens and all the equipment for the poultry farm at an auction. Anton eventually bought the land, which included everything from the top of the rock to Quarry Road.

Anton worked in the Raven Rock Quarry owned by Charlie Eastburn where he earned a steam engineer's license. In 1927, he bought the garage for car repair in Stockton, where he became famous for being able to fix everything. He was even involved with the rocket that was tested by Robert Goddard up on Duck's Flat, which is the area around near Route 519 near Sanford and Strimples Mill Road.

This same year, he married Bertha Klein (1897–1987), who had graduated as a nurse from Woman's Medical College of Philadelphia in 1921. From 1923 to 1925, she worked as a nurse in Liberia, Africa, with the Lutheran Mission.

The newlyweds had a grand plan for their honeymoon—Italy, France and Germany. They went by ship, of course. Frieda, Bertha's sister, came with them, and so did the Jewett—their six-cylinder, fifty-horsepower automobile made in Detroit.

In 1944, he bought the eighteenth-century Johnson houses and farm, including the quarry, between Federal Twist and the River Road. He

The Johnson Tenant House. *Courtesy of Luverne Updegrove Caulton.*

and Bertha were able to move in 1962 to this home, where they lived out the rest of their lives just a stone's throw from where he first started his life in America.

In 1951, Tony was told that the tenant house on the future Route 29 would have to be demolished unless he could move it, which he did, by himself, while the Naylor family still lived in it. With this action, Tony gave greater meaning to the phrase, "mover and shaker."

In 1961, they had another grand plan: drive the Pan-American Highway in their early '50s Micro Volkswagen Bus. They got as far as Santiago, Chile, where they encountered an earthquake that prompted them to board a freighter with the VW and return home.

HANNAH KERR UPDEGROVE (1909–1995)

Hannah Updegrove, an exemplary twentieth-century woman, was born in neighboring Kingwood and moved to Raven Rock with her family, who had lived and worked on several local farms, when she was fifteen.

After the death of her husband from a pulmonary embolism as a complication of influenza in 1932, Hannah came back home to live with her parents, Alvin and Annie Kerr. Thereafter, one-year-old Luverne and two-year-old Floyd were cared for by their grandparents, and Hannah became the primary earner.

Hannah had wanted to be a nurse. That would not happen, but she did find work as a caregiver to invalids for ten dollars per week. While working in Lumberville, Hannah walked home every night, but when she worked in Carversville, she came home for only two hours on Sundays.

Life in Raven Rock had its challenges: there was no electricity or indoor toilets (installed in 1993), water came from an outdoor hand pump (still in use today), drinking water had to be carried from the spring down the road; the floods of 1936 and 1955 proved devastating; a rutted farm track was the main thoroughfare out; and a five-mile round-trip walk to the one room Reading school was required for Floyd and Luverne and their friends, the Scarboros. Yet there were good times, too. Uncle Kimble and Aunt Eliza lived next door and ran the post office and general store. There was an occasional chicken brought from Cousin Willard, who worked on the farm on the road to Rosemont. There was food from the garden and good berry picking. And there were the rides in the Reo Flying Cloud, Floyd Updegrove's legacy to his family.

Other opportunities for adventure were the canal, the river and the railroad with the excitement it brought to their doorstep. Luverne remembered the train car full of young men going off to war and a note with a name thrown to her. The circus train would stop during the night, and the sounds of the animals could be heard. Later, the train would take the young folks to high school in Lambertville. When the covered bridge was closed to pedestrians in 1944, Floyd rowed Hannah, his mom, across the river to her work. She could not swim, and she did not have a life preserver. Others who needed to get to the other side also trusted their lives to young Floyd. Floyd went on to serve his country, build his own home and work until he was eighty-one.

Hannah worked for Diamond Silver in Lambertville until it closed in 1954. Finally, she joined her daughter and another Raven Rock resident, Sue Kintzel, at Belmont Forwarders, a glassware shipping company in Lambertville. She retired at age seventy-nine.

AND THE MANY OTHERS

To note the obvious, no person is without interest. It is with regret that only a few abbreviated tales of Raven Rock residents are recorded here.

You will read about Barbara Coar again since she was such a colorful, charismatic, diverse and sometimes charming activist. Sam Waugh remembered as a boy scout in the 1960s assembling in Barbara's home, the old post office. She handed them a bag lunch and a placard and then drove them off to the Delaware Water Gap, where they became part of the historic saving of Sunfish Pond.

Before Barbara had plumbing and while she was still going to New York City to work, it is said that she would bathe in the quarry and dress

Ashbel Welch, the genius who designed the D&R Canal and then went on to direct the Belvidere & Delaware Railroad, a branch of the Pennsylvania Railroad, in the nineteenth century. *Collection of Jeff Adams.*

while running to catch the train. Perhaps this was a ploy to keep the train from leaving without her.

More than any other person, the importance of Raven Rock rests on the genius of Ashbel Welch. This canal and railroad builder, corporate manager, industrial designer, inventor, and marine architect had an incredible career as a most proficient and innovative engineer. He was responsible for the construction of the feeder canal, which starts at Bull's Island. This masterpiece survives today as the seventy-mile Delaware & Raritan Canal Park. It is speculated that he might have been associated with the mysterious unnamed structure next to the Raven Rock Railroad Station. Ashbel Welch had an impressive brick home in Lambertville at the corner of Union and York Streets, but he certainly had land interests in Raven Rock since his name appears on period maps.

The Laszlos—George from Hungary and Edna from New York City—brought a new industry to Raven Rock: the manufacture of the Laszlo Fine Art Printing Press. They also brought with them a little of the high life of Manhattan. They had big plans for a Raven Rock Resort; fortunately or unfortunately, this never got off the drawing board.

B.A. Sorby a graduate of William and Mary College, bought the house just under the rock, known as Raven Rock House, in 1948. He was the county historian and a tireless worker who made things happen. But mostly, he would never let us forget the history of his beloved Raven Rock.

During World War II, Max and Wanda Tusche arrived and began to buy properties, eventually five, in Raven Rock and on Bull's Island. Son Rudy and Doris were married on the Tusche lawn and, for a time, ran one of the stores in Lumberville. Luverne Updegrove Caulton told of the day she headed off to New York City in an ice storm; she got as far as Rudy's place, where she ended up facing his stone wall. Once he established that she wanted to go back home, he braced himself against the wall and, with his good leg, pushed the car around.

The ongoing Emmons tenure began with the marriage of Ella and Asher Emmons in about 1905. The births of Arleigh, Sara and Florence deepened the roots on their farm on the south side of Federal Twist. Asher's younger brother, George, with his wife, May, moved into the house just north of the rock, securing central Raven Rock. George was a carpenter, a mason, a beekeeper, a gardener, a well-rounded man and an artisan, ready to share knowledge and tools with all. He was most remembered for propagating and maintaining the magnificent wisteria that drew throngs to the rock in the spring. The cliff, the house and the wisteria were blasted away to make room for the new road in 1960.

Arleigh and Ethel were married in 1942. Arleigh received three U.S. Navy Stars for his work on warship turbines at DeLaval in Trenton. Ethel and one of their three children, along with a grandson and his family, still live on Federal Twist. Ethel, at present a seventy-year resident of Raven Rock, has been a valuable asset in the Delaware Township oral history project.

George Emmons's famous wisteria vine climbing the "Raven Rock." Tourists and artists came to see the vine in bloom to photograph and paint it. *Courtesy of Luverne Updegrove Caulton.*

According to Doug McMichael, Bull's Island was a fantastic place to grow up. And he should know since he lived on the island from age six to seventeen, until the state claimed the land and he and his family moved to Rosemont. The island has a long tradition of recreation. In the 1890s, it was fitted out as a place for picnics under the name "Elmaker Island." At that time, it was easily accessible by train since it was also the station. When Doug lived here, there was an established campground. It was a poignant event when Doug's friend Sam Waugh, as a summer employee in 1972, helped with the removal of Doug's home, making way for the Delaware & Raritan Canal State Park. The D&R Park is truly special—in fact, it is one of our greatest environmental and recreational assets—but it should be noted that for the good of the many, individuals have sacrificed.

The eighteenth-century Quinby house, now know as Stone Rows Farm, has been managed by Walter Zdepski for the past forty years. During this time, Mr. Zdepski, a lifelong resident on Federal Twist Road, has overseen the transition from working farm to preserved farmland.

RAVEN ROCK GOING FORWARD

It takes more than a few persons of interest to raise a village. Those persons usually come equipped with family and friends who foster and cultivate the drive and energy it takes to build a home and neighborhood. Raven Rock was always a place for new arrivals. Whether they came from Rosemont or Hungary, they brought new life to the old rock. And still they come.

Each person continues to contribute in his or her own unique manner to the village, and it is this collective offering that creates the community. Sometimes it happens that a family arrives and grows and pours more than the figurative blood, sweat and tears into the commonwealth. Some have already been recorded. Here is one more but undoubtedly not the last. On July 4, 1983, Hidden Valley Nursery arrived. Hattie and Paul Dorko began their stewardship of two nineteenth-century homes formerly belonging to the Emmons and Schuck families. They raised their five children and grew their business from the land. True to Raven Rock tradition, they incorporated a splash of artistry into the mix with the mother and daughter combo owning and operating Charles Tiles of Sergeantsville. And thanks to son Ian, along Daniel Bray Highway can be seen the beginnings of a new venture for Raven Rock: a vineyard.

About the Editor

R. Curt Chinnici is a schoolteacher and author. He holds an art history degree from the University of Delaware and a Master's Degree in historic preservation from the Savannah College of Art & Design. He has published on Argand lighting and King of Prussia marble in *Antiques* magazine and for the Chipstone Foundation. He has also co-authored an Arcadia book with author Jeffrey Adams. He and Adams bought a home in Raven Rock, New Jersey, and soon met local historians who encouraged them to join the history society in Delaware Township, New Jersey. This group met and conceived of the idea for *Stories from Raven Rock, New Jersey*, with nine local historians contributing articles for this book project.